THE BEATLES'
LIVERPOOL

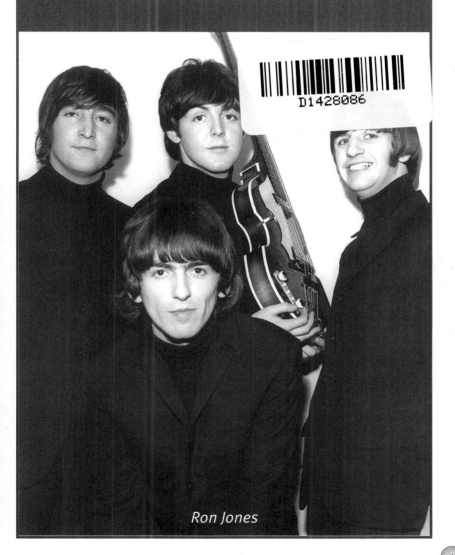

D1428086

Ron Jones

This book is dedicated, with love, to my long-suffering wife, Ann, my two fine children, Alison and Richard, and Amber, my adorable grand-daughter.

This edition published July 2000

First published in Great Britain 1991.

Copyright ©1991 and 2000 Ron Jones

All rights reserved. No part of this publication may be reproduced, stored in or introduced into a retrieval system, or transmitted, in any form or by any means (electronic, mechanical, photocopying, recording or otherwise), without the prior written permission of the copyright holder and publisher of this book.

ISBN 0–9511703–3–3

Designed, produced and published by
Ron Jones Associates
Suite 1, Egerton House
Tower Road
Birkenhead
Wirral
CH41 1FN

e-mail: ron@merseywide.demon.co.uk

For Liverpool…
Birthplace of The Beatles

There are places I'll remember all my life,
Though some have changed,
Some forever, not for better,
Some have gone and some remain.

All these places had their moments,
With lovers and friends I still can recall,
Some are dead and some are living,
In my life I've loved them all.

"In My Life" John Lennon and Paul McCartney
With acknowledgements to Northern Songs Ltd.

Liddypool *('Liverpool' by John Lennon)*

This visitor's guide to 'Liddypool' (Liverpool) by John Lennon appeared in his book 'In His Own Write', although it was first published in the 'Mersey Beat' newspaper:

"Reviving the old tradition of Judro Bathing is slowly but slowly dancing in Liddypool once more. Had you remembering these owld custard of Boldy Street blowing? The Peer Hat is very popularce for sun eating and Boots for Nude Brighter is handys when sailing. We are not happy with her Queen Victorious Monologue, but Walky Through Gallery is goodly when the rain and Sit Georgie House is black (and white from the little pilgrims flying from Hellsy College). Talk Hall is very histerical with old things wot are fakes and King Anne never slept there I tell you. Shout Airborne is handly for planes if you like (no longer government patrolled) and the L.C.C.C. (Liddypool Cha Cha Cha) are doing a great thing. The Mersey Boat is selling another three copies to some go home foreigners who went home.
There is a lot to do in Liddypool, but not all convenience."

But what does it all mean? As Paul McCartney said in the introduction to John's book..."None of it has to make sense, and if it seems funny then that's enough."

Here's my interpretation although I haven't a clue what his first sentence means!

Can you remember the old custom of Bold Street blowing? The Pier Head is very popular for sun bathing and boats are handy for sailing to New Brighton. We are not happy with the Queen Victoria Monument, but the Walker Art Gallery is good when it's raining and St George's Hall is black (and white from the little pigeons). Speke Hall is very historical with old things that are fakes and I can tell you that Queen Anne never slept there. Speke Airport is handy if you like planes (it's no longer government controlled) and Liverpool City Council are doing a great job. The 'Mersey Beat' is selling another three copies to some "Go home foreigners!" who went home.
There is a lot to do in Liverpool, but not all of it is convenient.

Contents

BIRTHPLACE OF THE BEATLES

The year is 1961. The Cuban heels on your winklepicker shoes clack noisily on the wet cobblestones. You turn up the collar on your short, 'bum freezer', jacket to keep out the cold March wind that whips through this narrow canyon of a street flanked by age-blackened warehouses.

Light, and sound, spill from an open doorway. You head towards it. Excitement grips your stomach. You edge past the bulky frame of doorman Paddy Delaney who nods approval at the membership card held up for inspection. Carefully, for they are worn and steep, you descend, with quickening heartbeat, the 18 stone steps into the blackness below.

As you reach the bottom, it hits you like a sledgehammer. The wall of heat given off by a multitude of perspiring bodies. That odour, a mixture of cheap disinfectant, sweat, cigarette smoke and the mustiness of ancient cellars. The catacomb darkness pierced by a few naked light bulbs.

And the sound. Especially the sound. That all-consuming sound that sears the brain. The driving rhythm hacked out on the Rickenbacker, the melody robustly overlaid by the Gretsch. Underpinning it, the booming Hofner violin bass and, binding it all together, the unrelenting beat punched out on the drums.

You elbow a pathway through to the centre of the three aisles and look over the sea of bobbing heads, willing your eyes to cut through the fug to see who is producing that unique, exciting sound. As if confirmation were necessary. It could only come from one source.

Four figures clad in worn black leathers and sweat-sodden tee-shirts dominate the tiny wooden stage which threatens to shatter beneath the sheer power of the beat that is their hallmark. All eyes are fixed on the lead singer. Legs apart, hunched over his Rickenbacker, the microphone is but a whisper away from his lips. Through tortured vocal cords comes a raw sound which, despite the inferno-like heat, causes you to shiver... "You make me dizzy Miss Lizzy, with your rock and roll..."

Yes. This is the Cavern, Mathew Street. On stage is the greatest rock and roll band the world has ever known...The Beatles!

And this is Liverpool, 'City of The Beatles' YEAH! YEAH! YEAH!

Pier Head, Liverpool 1961

WALKING IN THE FOOTSTEPS OF THE BEATLES IN LIVERPOOL CITY CENTRE

Set out on the pages that follow is a grand Liverpool City Centre Beatles trail. All of the important Beatle places and most of the tourist sights in the City Centre are included on this walk.

Not allowing for any stops, it should take less than two hours to follow this trail. I suggest you start at the Albert Dock where there is ample free parking, toilets, lots of eating and drinking places and a Tourist Information Centre. Added to that it's Liverpool's No 1 visitor attraction, home to The Beatles Story and a starting point for the Magical Mystery Bus Tour (see page 100). What more could you possibly want?! The trail ends at the Queen Square Tourist Information Centre (see page 100). Alternatively, if it's more convenient, you could just as easily start there and finish at Albert Dock – simply follow the trail in reverse order.

Remember to bring your camera and plenty of film. There are lots of interesting Beatle landmarks and great views of the city to photograph.

Happy walking!

HELP!

Please respect the privacy of the people who live in the houses mentioned in these Beatles trails.

Don't disturb them by knocking on their doors, peeping through their windows or otherwise trespassing on their property. The Beatles left Liverpool long ago and none of their families now live in any of these houses.

Great care has been taken to make sure that the information in this book is correct. However, Liverpool is a restless, changing city. Many of the Beatle places featured in the first edition of this book, published in 1991, either don't exist now or have changed radically. The process continues to this day. Come back tomorrow and it will have changed again!

Pier Head, Liverpool 2000

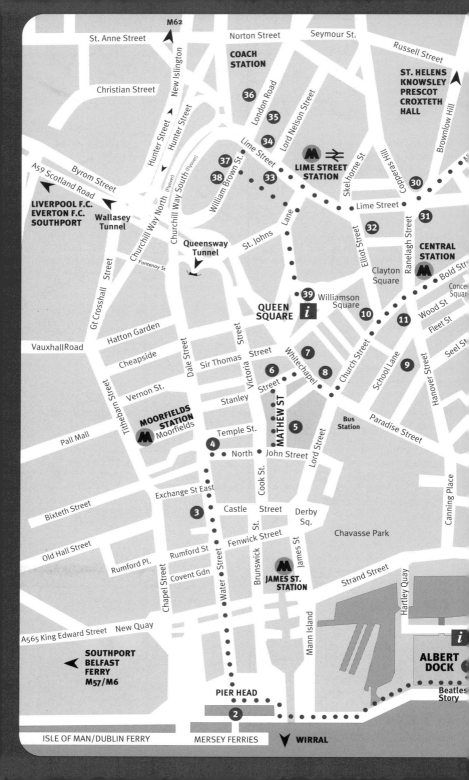

IN THE FOOTSTEPS OF THE BEATLES
LIVERPOOL CITY CENTRE

1. Albert Dock/Beatles Story
2. Pier Head/Mersey Ferries
3. Liverpool Town Hall
4. Former Cassanova Club
5. Cavern Quarter – see p13
6. Eleanor Rigby sculpture
7. Rushworth's Music Store
8. Former NEMS
9. Bluecoat Chambers
10. Former Reeces Restaurant
11. Neptune Theatre
12. Jacaranda
13. Former Mersey Beat Office
14. Blue Angel Club
15. Liverpool Cathedral
16. 3 Gambier Terrace
17. 7 Percy Street
18. Former College of Art
19. Former Liverpool Institute
20. Ye Cracke Pub
21. 36 Falkner Street
22. Philharmonic Hall
23. Former Children's Hospital
24. Philharmonic Pub
25. Everyman Theatre
26. Former Maternity Hospital
27. R.C. Cathedral
28. 4 Rodney Street
29. 64 Mount Pleasant
30. Adelphi Hotel
31. Lewis's Store
32. Former Blacklers Store
33. St George's Hall
34. Empire Theatre
35. Odeon Cinema
36. Former Cassanova Club
37. Walker Art Gallery
38. Picton Library
39. Queen Square T.I.C.

STARTING POINT: ALBERT DOCK/THE BEATLES STORY

No visitor to Liverpool should leave the city without first visiting the Albert Dock, and not just because it is the home of The Beatles Story. The converted warehouses, dating from 1846, form the largest group of Grade One 'listed' buildings (on

account of their historical and architectural importance) in Britain. It is also the most popular heritage attraction in the country, pulling in over four million visitors a year. The Albert Dock is visually stunning and a very pleasant place in which to spend the day.

The complex is a mixture of speciality shops, restaurants and bars, and top-class visitor attractions

Paul, Linda and band in pre-concert photo call at Albert Dock.

which include the Tate Gallery Liverpool and the Merseyside Maritime Museum where, in the HM Customs & Excise National Museum on the ground floor, you can see gold discs for the single *A Hard Day's Night* and the LP *Something New*, destined for presentation to the Beatles but seized by Customs Officers because the duty had not been paid on them.

In the basement of Britannia Pavilion is The Beatles Story which opened in April 1990. The Beatles Story is literally that...the story of the Beatles from their childhood days through to their break-up and the pursuit of individual careers. This is done by way of a series of set pieces such as the office of the Mersey Beat newspaper, Hamburg's Reeperbahn, the Cavern, the Yellow Submarine, a Lennon 'White Room' etc. There is also a souvenir shop. *(Open daily from 10am)*

On permanent display are eleven cartoon drawings produced in 1978 by Cynthia Lennon to illustrate her autobiography *A Twist of Lennon* and purchased by the Beatles Story in 1999. Another new addition that year was a replica of the Casbah Coffee Club (see also page 75).

Paul proudly wears his Liver Bird badge during his magical dockland concert. The Liver Bird is the official symbol of Liverpool and dates back to the founding of the city by King John nearly 800 years ago.

The daily Beatles sightseeing tours, run in a replica of the original Magical Mystery Tour bus, set off from the Beatles Story and tours are also run from here to Paul McCartney's former house at 20 Forthlin Road *(Enquiries - Tel: 0151 708 8574)*.

Kings Dock, immediately south of the Albert Dock, was the setting for a fabulous sell-out open air concert staged by Paul on the evening of 28th June 1990.

(Exit Albert Dock by the Tate Gallery, cross the bridge and take the Riverside Walkway to the Pier Head. N.B. This walkway closes in the evening so you will have to leave by the main Albert Dock exit and walk along the dock road to the Pier Head.)

THE PIER HEAD/MERSEY FERRIES

Departure point for the famous Mersey Ferries. The Pier Head and its landmark buildings, the 'Three Graces' – the Cunard Building, Port of Liverpool Building and especially the Royal Liver Building topped by the mythical twin Liver Birds – are powerful emotional symbols of the city for all Liverpudlians, or Scousers as we are sometimes called.

It has always been an especially favourite place for Liverpool children and the Beatles were no exception. They would be drawn here to marvel at the giant transatlantic liners which were such a glamorous feature of the Pier Head until the early 1970's. No doubt too they rode on the now-demolished Overhead Electric Railway, the world's first, and nick-named 'The Docker's Umbrella', which gave them a bird's eye view of the then booming Liverpool docks stretching from Dingle in the south to Seaforth in the north.

John, Paul, George and Ringo would travel here on bone-rattling 'Green Goddesses', Liverpool's much-missed electric trams, to catch the ferryboat that would take them across the fast-flowing River Mersey to the funfair and sands at New Brighton or the beaches at Wallasey

The ferry to New Brighton has long gone but you can still savour one of the truly essential Liverpool experiences – a short cruise on one of the famous old Mersey Ferries. The ferries are immortalised in the Gerry and the Pacemakers song *Ferry 'cross the Mersey* which, along with their other hit *You'll never walk alone* have virtually become twin anthems for Liverpool.

The Beatles on board the 'Salvor' at the Pier Head. The ship's mast is now a feature of the traffic island between the Royal Liver Building and the Crowne Plaza hotel.

Yoko and Sean at the Pier Head during their 1984 'pilgrimage' to the city John loved so much.

Launched in 1951, the *Royal Iris* had been the most high profile of the Mersey Ferries 'fleet' for some 40 years. Intended as an up-market dance-cruise ship, she became known to one and all as the 'fish and chip boat'. It was as such that the Beatles performed on board her during 1960 and 1961 in four 'Riverboat Shuffles' presented by the Cavern. Judged too expensive to repair, she was eventually pensioned off.

The Pier Head was also the venue for a controversial Lennon concert on 5th May 1990 promoted by Yoko Ono who appeared on stage with Sean and a host of pop luminaries. Performers as diverse as Lou Reed, Cyndi Lauper, Randy Travis and Kylie Mynogue performed cover versions of Lennon hits with varying degrees of success to a less-than-capacity audience.

However, the event did raise more than £300,000 for the University of Liverpool to set up a scholarship fund to help needy students. A video of the concert *Lennon: A Tribute* was released in April 1991.

(Turn right at the equestrian statue of King Edward VII and go between the Royal Liver and Cunard Buildings. At the traffic lights, cross the dock road into Water Street which contains a number of fine buildings, principally India Building, Oriel Chambers and Martins Bank Building. At the top of Water Street, jutting out into the road, is the Town Hall)

LIVERPOOL TOWN HALL *Water Street*
BEATLES' CIVIC RECEPTION

As they stood on the balcony alongside the Lord Mayor and other civic dignitaries, the Beatles received a hero's welcome from the tens of thousands of their Merseyside fans who crowded the streets fanning out from the Town Hall.

Earlier on that Friday evening, 10 July 1964, they had headed a cavalcade cheered by nearly a quarter of a million fans as it slowly made its way from Speke Airport to the city centre and the glittering civic reception that awaited them.

From the Minstrel's Gallery, the Beatles gazed down on the specially invited guests assembled to pay homage to them in the ballroom of the City's beautiful Georgian Town Hall, built in 1754. In the intimacy of the Lord Mayor's Parlour they sipped tea from china cups elegantly embossed with Liverpool's Coat of Arms.

Later that evening, to yet more scenes of Beatlemania, they attended the northern premiere of their first film *A Hard Day's Night* at the Odeon Cinema in London Road. They had well and truly 'arrived' in the city of their birth.

In the Council Chamber on the ground floor the City Council passed the resolution that confirmed the honour of Freemen of the City on the Beatles. Their names are inscribed on the list of Honorary Freemen in the Entrance Hall. Public openings are arranged every year – highly recommended.

(Continue along Dale St. Cross the lights at North John St. On the next block is The Temple)

CASSANOVA CLUB *The Temple, Dale Street*

Named after popular Merseybeat group, Cass and the Cassanovas, the Cassanova Club was housed for a short time in an upstairs room in the Temple building. Here on a Sunday afternoon early in 1960 the Beatles played during the interval.

(Return to North John St., continue down the street and cross at the junction with Victoria St.)

THE CAVERN QUARTER:

MATHEW STREET

The Mathew Street you see today is nothing like the grubby little warehouse street of the Merseybeat era. Nowadays it is part of the trendy 'Cavern Quarter' pub and club scene and has well and truly cashed in on its Beatles heritage. Apart from the Cavern club and Cavern Walks complex, you will find a John Lennon Bar, Rubber Soul pub, and Beatles Shop. Even the humble electricity sub-station has had a make-over! There is also is a Cavern Pub which has one of the Hofner bass guitars made famous by Paul. "Cool Cavern. Paul McCartney Dec 14 '99" he wrote on the scratchplate.

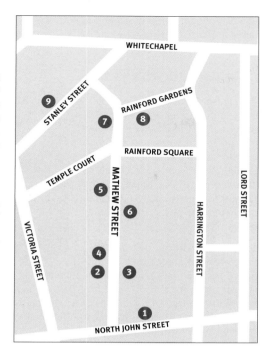

1) CENTRAL BUILDINGS

Cavern City Tours, who have been responsible for numerous Beatles initiatives over the years, plan to develop a *Hard Day's Night* Beatles themed hotel in this building which occupies the entire block from Mathew Street to Harrington Street.

2) CAVERN PUB/WALL OF FAME/LENNON STATUE

Billy J Kramer and Gerry share a laugh. The statue has since undergone a head transplant and now sports a mop top...and still looks nothing like John!

The 40th anniversary of the Cavern was celebrated in style on 16 January 1997 with a huge birthday bash. A *Wall of Fame* formed of bricks etched with the names of the 1,801 bands who played the club between 1957 and 1973 was unveiled by Gerry Marsden of Gerry and the Pacemakers. Billy J Kramer unveiled a statue which bears little resemblance to John Lennon. The Cavern Pub opened in 1994 and is themed around the famous bands and stars who played at the Cavern including The Rolling Stones, The Who, Chuck Berry, Jimi Hendrix and, of course, the Beatles.

Also planned for Mathew Street is a 'Wall of Hits' to commemorate the 50 plus local bands and artistes who have had No.1. hit records since 1953.

3) THE CAVERN/CAVERN WALKS

The stylish Cavern Walks complex opened in Spring 1984 and replaced a row of grimy old warehouses. In one of these, number ten, formerly a wine and spirit store, egg packing station and even a makeshift air raid shelter against Hitler's Luftwaffe, 18 stone steps led down to a cellar club the name of which was to become known the world over. That club was the Cavern.

Here, in the catacombed darkness beneath your feet, the Beatles played no less than 274 times. They made their debut during the lunchtime of 21 February 1961 for £5 and went on to play a further 151 lunchtime sessions. Their final performance, for £300, took place on the evening of Saturday 3 August 1963. Along with other top local groups, for the Mersey Sound was never just the Beatles, they made the Cavern the most famous rock and roll venue of its day.

But the Cavern had not always echoed to the big beat sound. When doctor's son Alan Sytner bought it in 1956 he planned a similar venture to 'Le Caveau Francais', the Parisian jazz club. The Cavern first opened its doors to a jazz-only crowd on 16 January 1957, but soon yielded to the skiffle craze sweeping the country at that time. It was to be the thin end of a very large rock and roll wedge.

Indeed, it was as the Quarry Men skiffle group that the young Beatles made their first true appearance at the Cavern on 7 August 1957. Paul missed this historic event. He was away at a Boy Scout Summer camp at the time. And six months were to pass before the 14 year old George Harrison was to meet the Quarry Men for the first time. The original 1957 Quarry Men line-up (minus John Lennon and of course it wasn't the *real* Cavern) played their first gig at the Cavern almost 42 years to the day of their debut appearance.

Maggie May, Railroad Bill, Cumberland Gap and other Lonnie Donegan skiffle numbers would have been been as much a part of the Beatles' repertoire in those days as their distinctive versions of Elvis, Chuck Berry and Buddy Holly classics. However, by this time, the first hesitant efforts of the Lennon/McCartney song-writing partnership were also being given an airing.

Don't you rock me Daddy-O

In 1959 the Cavern passed into the hands of accountant Ray McFall. Although rock and roll had occasionally sneaked in, much to the disgust of the regular jazz purists, it was not until 25 May 1961 that McFall relented to allow the very first beat night. On stage that night were the immensely popular Cass and the Cassanovas (later the Big Three) and Rory Storm and the Hurricanes whose drummer was none other than Ringo Starr. From that night the Cavern was 'lost' to rock and roll.

Welcoming fans to 'the best of cellars', the Cavern's legendary DJ, Bob Wooler, the 'Prince of Pun', introduced the cream of the hundreds of Merseyside groups that had emerged out of the short-lived skiffle boom – the

Bob Wooler: living legend and embodiment of the Cavern and Merseybeat..

Searchers, the Swinging Blue Jeans, the Remo Four, Gerry and the Pacemakers, Billy J Kramer and the Dakotas, the Fourmost, the Big Three and, of course, the Beatles. And there was a girl singer, the Cavern's cloakroom attendant Priscilla White, better known as Cilla Black.

'Legends in their own lunchtime'

On 9 November 1961, during one of its famous lunchtime sessions, a sober-suited 27 year old Brian Epstein visited the Cavern to see for himself its star performers, the Beatles. He watched. He listened. He was hooked. Despite the warnings of Allan Williams, their so-called first manager, "not to touch them with an effing barge-pole", the besotted Brian eventually signed them up in his NEMS office in nearby Whitechapel on Wednesday 24 January 1962.

Cavern of Dreams

Amid howls of protest, the debt-ridden Cavern was closed down by the Official Receiver on 28 February 1966. It was ceremoniously re-opened five months later on 23 July by Prime Minister Harold Wilson who was presented with a wooden pipe crafted from the original stage which had been broken up in 1964 and sold piece by piece for charity.

Although it survived for another seven years, it closed its doors for the last time on 27 May 1973 as Paul McCartney and his new group Wings played the final night of their UK tour at the Odeon Cinema, Hammersmith. The warehouse was then bulldozed to the ground to provide a working site for the construction of Liverpool's new underground railway system. Most Beatle fans are amazed that the City of Liverpool did nothing to stop this act of cultural vandalism. And who can blame them?

For a number of years the historic Cavern site was an unsightly temporary car park before it was bought by the Liverpool-based company Royal Life (now Royal & Sun Alliance) and redeveloped into the Cavern Walks shops and offices complex that you see today.

The Cavern Lives!

Cavern Walks bristles with Beatle features. Cynthia Lennon designed the terracotta embellishments to its frontage. Cavern Mecca, the Beatles fan centre which had been living a hand to mouth existence in another old warehouse in Mathew Street, was given a new, if short-lived, home here. (It folded the following year). It had as its centre-piece the Yellow Submarine specially built for the premiere of the film. Perhaps inappropriately for Liverpool, there is even an Abbey Road pub. Equally inappropriate in my view is the 'official' statue to the Fab Four by John Doubleday, unveiled by a nonplussed Mike McCartney who quizzed…"Which one's our kid?!"

Most exciting of all, the Cavern club was rebuilt as near to the original as possible using bricks saved from the old Cavern. Whilst it is not an exact replica and can never recapture the magical atmosphere of the original Cavern, it is worth a visit since it's the nearest thing to the real Cavern that you can experience.

The highspot for the 'new' Cavern came on 14th December 1999 when Paul performed his last gig of the millennium here in front of 150 lucky fans and a similar number of media people. Paul explained - "I am going back for just one night as a nod to the music that has and will ever thrill me. I can't think of a better way to rock out the end of the century than with a rock 'n' roll gig at the Cavern."

The street is also the main focus for the Mathew Street Festival which takes place every August and attracts many thousands of people.

4) ARTHUR DOOLEY'S BEATLE SCULPTURE

You'll either love or loathe this celebration of the Fab Four by local sculptor the late Arthur Dooley, a giant of a man with a larger-than-life character to match. When it was erected in 1974, this curious dedication to the 'Four Lads Who Shook The World' consisted of four cherubic images fashioned from plastic dolls. One, Paul, has disappeared and a plaque explains, punfully, that 'Paul has taken wings and flown.' A guitar-carrying cherub complete with a 'Lennon Lives' halo was added in 1980.

5) THE GRAPES PUB

'The Beatles' Pub', as it is known, is opposite the Cavern and therefore the obvious choice for the Beatles and other Merseybeat groups. It was a popular refuge from the Cavern where coffee or Coca Cola were the strongest drinks on offer. Here the Beatles would down pints of Brown Mix or Black Velvet and Brian, when he did join them, decorously sipped brandy. When Pete Best was sacked from the Beatles on 16 August 1962, he drowned his sorrows here with their Road Manager, Neil Aspinall.

6) ELECTRICITY SUB-STATION

Unremarkable during the daytime, this humble electricity sub-station comes to life at night when passers-by are treated to a fascinating computer-controlled light show complete with swirling Sixties psychedelic colours and a yellow submarine scudding across the walls of the adjoining buildings.

7) THE BEATLES SHOP

The only shop in Liverpool dedicated to selling Beatles memorabilia and nothing else. In fact they claim to stock the largest range of Beatle merchandise in the world. Above the doorway is a sculpture by local artist David Hughes which is unique in being the only one in Liverpool which looks remotely like the Beatles. Look out too for the specially-commissioned Beatles carpet inside the shop.

Visitors to the shop have included Sean Lennon, Beatles producer George Martin, Neil Aspinall, head of Apple, and Ringo who popped in to use their telephone! *Enquiries – Tel: 0151 236 8066.*

To the left of the shop is the Mathew Street Gallery, opened in 1999 which specialises in the art of John Lennon. *Enquiries – Tel: 0150 236 0009.*

(From here look down Rainford Gardens and you will see The White Star pub next door to the Quarter Cafe Bar)

8) WHITE STAR PUB *Button Street*

Mecca for drinkers of Draft Bass, the White Star was an alternative venue to the Grapes pub for the Beatles and the other groups appearing at the Cavern.

(Walk to the end of Mathew Street, look to the left and across the street you will see the Eleanor Rigby sculpture set back from the railings.)

9) ELEANOR RIGBY STATUE *Stanley Street*

Dedicated to 'all the lonely people'... the mythical, sad figure in the Beatles' famous song, was sculpted by Tommy 'I've never felt more like singing the blues' Steele as a tribute to the Liverpudlian pop idols.

In the certain knowledge that the City Fathers would not put their hands in their pockets for any memorial to the Beatles,Tommy gave it to them for half a sixpence, just over one penny. History has not recorded whether or not he ever received payment. I suspect not. The actual cost of casting the statue in bronze was met by the Liverpool Echo, the newspaper which claims to have coined the term 'Merseybeat'. Almost as interesting as the statue itself is what Tommy enigmatically placed inside it...a four leaf clover for luck; a page from the Bible for spiritual help; a sonnet for lovers; an adventure book for excitement and a pair of football boots for action.

On 3 December 1982 the perky Cockney performed the official unveiling of his creation, explaining – "I put them all inside the statue so she would be full of magical properties. I give Eleanor to Liverpool with an open heart and many thanks for my happy times in the City".

(Retrace your steps and near the bottom of Stanley Street on the right hand side is the former Hessy's music store.)

FORMER HESSY'S *(Now Wade Smith) Stanley Street*

One of Liverpool's two major musical instrument stores during the Merseybeat years presided over by the ever-present Frank Hessy and his star salesman Jim Gretty. The price of buying a guitar included a three-chord 'lesson' from Jim, a club performer himself. It was Jim who had sold John his first 'proper' £15 guitar in 1957.

One of Brian Epstein's early acts as their manager was to clear the £200 debt which the Beatles owed Hessy's for John's Hofner Club 40 guitar, George's Futurama guitar and Paul's amplification equipment.

Hessy's later featured in the film *Ferry 'cross the Mersey*.

On the corner of the street, next door to Hessy's, which closed its doors for the last time in 1995, was another Liverpool institution, the Kardomah Coffee House, a regular, non-alcoholic hangout for the Beatles.

(At the bottom of Stanley Street, if you look to the left you will see Rushworth's and if you look to the right you will see the Ann Summers shop.)

RUSHWORTH'S MUSIC HOUSE *Whitechapel*

Although a shadow of its former self, Rushworth's still claim to be Liverpool's largest musical instrument suppliers. Many of the Merseybeat groups, including the Beatles, bought their gear here. Their much-prized Gibson acoustic-electric guitars were specially flown in from Chicago and formally presented to them by James Rushworth the firm's Chairman. John always lamented that his favourite Gibson had somehow gone 'missing' on one of their later tours.

FORMER NEMS
(Now an Ann Summers shop)
12 Whitechapel

Legend has it that, on 28 October 1961, a youth called Raymond Jones walked into this NEMS record store and asked, without success, for *My Bonnie* by the Beatles. He had heard the record, a scorching rocker, at Hambleton Hall also known as the 'Hive of Jive', played by promoter/DJ Bob Wooler.

Wooler had encouraged his youthful audience to ask for it at their record shops. Teenager Raymond Jones took his advice and asked Brian Epstein for the record at this store. Epstein prided himself on being able to search out any record asked for by his customers and eventually tracked down the elusive record which subsequently turned out to be a minor best seller for him. Curious to find out more about the group that he claimed he'd never heard of before, he decided to visit the nearby Cavern club on 9 November 1961 when the Beatles were making one of their regular lunch-time appearances. The rest, as they say, is history.

It has since been suggested that Epstein was fully aware of the Beatles' popularity months before Raymond Jones asked him for their record. Surely, it is argued, the astute Epstein could not have avoided seeing the prominent coverage given to the Beatles on the front covers of *Mersey Beat*, the newspaper for which he both wrote reviews and sold in his store, or the dance tickets sold by NEMS which bore the Beatles' name.

The upstairs office here soon became the nerve centre for Brian's burgeoning NEMS Enterprises of which the Beatles were central.

By the Summer of 1963 the meteoric growth of NEMS Enterprises had led to the office being re-located from here to first floor premises above the Wizard's Den joke

shop at 24 Moorfields, a few streets away. In March of the following year Brian moved the entire NEMS Enterprises operation to London.

(Continue to the end of Whitechapel to Church Street. McDonald's has replaced Horne Brothers the gentlemen's outfitters in the basement of which was a barber shop where Brian Epstein sent the Beatles as part of his smarten up plan. Opposite, in Lord Street, was Times Furnishing where Brian served a six month sales apprenticeship for a weekly wage of £5 when he was 18 years old. Turn left into Church Street. (As you reach Littlewoods store on the right, look up Church Alley where you will see Bluecoat Chambers facing you.)

BLUECOAT CHAMBERS *School Lane*

Dating from 1717, this elegant Queen Anne building, the oldest in Liverpool city centre, is the legacy of a Liverpool slave trader and do-gooder...the city has always been a place of contradiction and controversy!

Long a centre for the arts, Yoko Ono appeared here on 26 September 1967 in a 'happening', a phenomenon of the 60's that now seems so daft. People sat dangling their legs over the stage eating sandwiches. The audience was invited to come on stage to chalk messages on a blackboard. And, as a climax, Yoko was bound to a chair with bandages and enveloped in smoke!

Less than a year earlier John had met Yoko for the first time at a private viewing of her avante-garde exhibition at London's Indica Gallery. Although he didn't know it at the time, he had met his soul mate.

In 1990 the Bluecoat staged an exhibition of works by Stuart Sutcliffe.

(Continue up Church Street to its junction, on the left, with Parker Street)

FORMER REECE'S RESTAURANT
(Above Superdrug store) Parker Street/Leigh Street

Reece's first floor restaurant was the unlikely venue for John and Cynthia's wedding breakfast on 23 August 1962. After their wedding in the Mount Pleasant Registry Office, they dashed through the pouring rain with Paul, George and Brian in tow to fight for a table along with dozens of other lunchtime shoppers. The set lunch of soup, roast chicken and trifle was paid for by Brian. The newly-weds were toasted with water since the restaurant was not licensed to serve alcohol.

(Continue to the end of Church Street. Opposite is Bold Street. To the right is Hanover Street where, on the next block along, is the Neptune Theatre.)

NEPTUNE THEATRE *Hanover Street*

In August 1997, on the 30th anniversary of Brian Epstein's death, Liverpool City Council dedicated this theatre to his memory. Paul remarked – "Brian would have loved this, to have a theatre in his name. He was always very keen on acting." Actually, Brian did buy a theatre of his own...the Saville in London's Shaftesbury Avenue in April 1965.

BOLD STREET

At the bottom of Bold Street, on the left, is the old Lyceum building which once housed Reece's Lyceum Cafe, something of a Liverpool institution but now sadly gone. It now houses a branch of the Co-operative Bank. The Beatles used to meet here for coffee and, it is said, pass the time composing songs on the backs of menus and table napkins.

(Half way up this street, on the right hand side, is Slater Street where, on the left hand side near its junction with Seel Street, is the Jacaranda Club.)

JACARANDA CLUB
23 Slater Street

Once owned by Allan Williams, the 'Jac' was a favourite place for the Beatles to hang out during their student days in the late 1950's. They would sit in the window playing their guitars, munching the Jac's famous bacon butties and making sarcastic remarks to the office girls coming in for a lunchtime snack. Downstairs, in the evening, the tiny airless basement reverberated to the then unlikely sound of the immensely popular 'Royal Caribbean' West Indian steel band. I can personally vouch that it was like the Black Hole of Calcutta, far sweatier than the Cavern!

The Beatles played about a dozen lunchtime and Monday evening engagements from May 1960 when the Royal Caribbean had their night off. Their payment? Coca Cola and beans on toast!

Also picture the scene on Tuesday, 15 August 1960 as the five Beatles, Allan Williams, his Chinese wife Beryl and her brother Barry Chang, and Allan's black friend 'Lord Woodbine', all crammed into Allan's battered old van and set off on their eventful journey to Hamburg.

The completely refurbished Jac reopened in 1996 with Pete and his Pete Best Band on stage. Pete commented – "It was in the Jacaranda that I first appeared with the

Beatles, just before they went over to Germany – it would have been way back in August 1960. We were so poor in those days, we had our girlfriends sitting in the front with mike stands strapped to broom handles. But it was excellent. It was the place to be; everyone used to arrange to meet up at the Jac."

Basement murals, supposedly painted by John and Stu Sutcliffe during their art student days, were restored in time for the re-opening.

(Retrace your steps to Bold Street and turn right.)

BOLD STREET *(continued)*

On the left hand side, at No 83, was Kaye Photography. When Brian Epstein needed new publicity photographs of the Beatles with the just-recruited Ringo he turned to one of Liverpool's best-known social photographers, Bill Connell, alias Peter Kaye. In those days Bill had a shop in Park Road and a modest studio in Newington, a rather shabby side street off Bold Street. Later he moved his operations to Bold Street, known in its heyday as 'The Bond Street of the North'. Those early historic images of the Beatles taken by Bill and his young assistant Les Chadwick in their studio, on derelict sites in Liverpool's docklands, in the Cavern and other Mersey Beat-era venues can be seen in Peter Kaye's *Beatles in Liverpool*, largely put together by Bill's assistant, Margaret Roberts, and published in 1987. Sadly, Bill, a flamboyant, larger-than-life character, died the following year and Apple has since bought the copyright of most of his photographs.

At number 89, near the top of the street, was the Odd Spot Club, venue for two Beatles gigs during 1962. Julia Lennon's partner, John Dykins, was once a waiter here.

(continue to the top of the street. To the left is Renshaw Street where, to the left on the opposite side of the road, is the former office of the Mersey Beat newspaper.)

81a RENSHAW STREET – FORMER OFFICE OF 'MERSEY BEAT'

The *Mersey Beat* newspaper was an avidly read guide to the local music scene produced by Bill Harry, an art college friend of John and Stu.

The front page of the first edition, published on 6 July 1961, featured a typically Lennonesque article under the headline – 'Being a Short Diversion on the Dubious Origins of the Beatles'. He explained how the Beatles came by their name...It came in a vision – a man appeared on a flaming pie and said unto them "From this day on you are Beatles with an A." *Flaming Pie* was also the title Paul gave to his 1997 album.

Until its demise some 90 editions later Bill's beat scene 'bible' recorded the Beatles' rise to fame. Frequent callers and regular contributors to *Mersey Beat*, which had its offices here above a wine merchant's shop next door to the Roscoe Arms pub, included the Beatles and Brian Epstein who reviewed records for the paper. During a Mersey Beat office move, a large bundle of John's stories and poems, written for the paper under his 'Beatcomber' pseudonym, managed to get 'lost'.

Another regular caller was Cavern DJ Bob Wooler who wrote a column called 'The Roving I'. The first article ever written about the Beatles was penned by Bob for Mersey Beat in mid-1961.

Nowadays Bill Harry is regarded as an authority on the Beatles. A prolific writer, he is the author of a number of books about the Beatles including *The Book of Lennon*, *The Beatles Who's Who*, and *The Beatles Encyclopedia*. Needless to say, copies of *Mersey Beat* are much sought after collector's items.

(At the top of Bold Street turn right into Berry Street. This marks the start of Liverpool's Chinatown, the oldest in Europe. Two streets along is Seel Street. Near the top, on the left is the Blue Angel club.)

BLUE ANGEL CLUB *108 Seel Street*

Previously called the Wyvern Social Club, this was the setting for two legendary auditions. In 1960, London rock impresario Larry Parnes was looking for a band to back his star protege Billy Fury. The Silver Beetles, with 'borrowed' drummer Johnny Hutchinson of Cass and the Cassanovas (later the Big Three), didn't pass the audition held on 10 May in the dingy basement...Stu's base playing was less than adequate. But they obviously impressed Parnes. He later hired them for a tour of Scotland with one of his other stars, Johnny Gentle.

Also watching the five groups being auditioned that day was Rory Storm, leader of Rory Storm and the Hurricanes, whose drummer was Ringo Starr.

Pete Best was drummer with his Casbah-based group the Blackjacks when Paul

telephoned that Summer to invite him to join the Beatles for their first trip to Hamburg. But first he had to audition here on 12 August 1960 prior to joining John, Paul, George and Stu as 'the Fifth Beatle'. Four days later they all set off for Hamburg.

The following year, now as the Blue Angel, the club was being run by the Beatles' 'manager' Allan Williams. The 'Blue' became *the* place for Liverpool musicians including the Beatles, although for a time Williams banned them from the club for non-payment of his manager's commission. It was also the natural choice for other stars visiting Liverpool. In those days you could have rubbed shoulders with the Rolling Stones, Bob Dylan, Judy Garland and, before she became famous, Cilla Black.

(Continue along Berry Street to the next set of traffic lights – note the spectacular Chinese arch…the biggest in Europe. To the right is Duke Street. Number 139 was once 'Joe's Cafe', a late night eating and meeting place during the Merseybeat era for the Beatles and other musicians. The owner, Joe Davy, subsequently became the owner of the Cavern during its declining years. Near the bottom of the street, at number 28, was the Cabaret Club which passed for sophistication in the Liverpool of the early 60's. The Beatles played here only once, on 25 July 1962, to an unappreciative audience. Cross left into Upper Duke Street.)

LIVERPOOL CATHEDRAL *Upper Duke Street/Hope Street*

This monumental building is the city's Anglican Cathedral, appropriately joined to its Catholic counterpart by a street called Hope. It was here that a Beatle was rejected because his singing voice was not good enough! In 1953 Paul McCartney auditioned here for a place in the cathedral choir but was unsuccessful. In a delicious touch of irony he returned in June 1991 for the world premiere of the partly-autobiographical *Liverpool Oratorio* the symphony he wrote in collaboration with Carl Davies to celebrate the 150th anniversary of the Royal Liverpool Philharmonic Orchestra.

It's an awe-inspiring building, the biggest cathedral in Britain and, after St John the Divine in New York, the largest Anglican cathedral in the world. On Sunday 29 March 1981 it became the fitting venue for a special memorial service when the people of Liverpool paid their official last respects to John Lennon. During this moving 'Festival of Peace' a selection of Lennon and McCartney songs was played on the cathedral's 10,000-pipe organ.

There are spectacular views over the city from the top of the 331ft tower and good food is served in the Refectory. It's an awesome building and a visit is a 'must'.

(As you walk up the hill, to the left you will see the rear of both the Liverpool Institute, now the Liverpool Institute for Performing Art, and the former College of Art – see pages 27-31. The next junction up the hill is Hope Street. From here, across the road to the right, and set back from the road, is Gambier Terrace)

3 GAMBIER TERRACE – JOHN'S FLAT

Much against his Aunt Mimi's advice, John left the comforts of 'Mendips' to share a flat here in 1960 with Stu Sutcliffe and Rod Murray, another student from art college. It was also a good place to spend time with Cynthia. Many was the night she spent here with John having hoodwinked her mother into believing she was staying over with a girlfriend.

The flat was an ideal place for John and Stu to draw and paint together and for the Beatles to rehearse; soon they would be off to Hamburg. Apparently, they lived in some squalor, something seized on by The People newspaper and used in a dramatic expose as an example of the 'Beatnik Horror' sweeping the country. It has since been revealed that the whole story was a put up job by the publicity-seeking Allan Williams, the Beatles' first 'manager'.

When John and Stu set off for Hamburg from here with the rest of the Beatles in Summer 1960, John left all his possessions in Rod Murray's flat. A year later he suggested to Rod that he should keep anything he wanted and throw the rest away. He kept only two items and in 1984 at Sotheby's Rock and Roll Memorabilia auction in London he sold one of John's school exercise books containing 16 pages of poetry, prose, drawings and cartoons for £16,000. The value, in both artistic and monetary terms, of the material thrown away by Rod does not bear thinking about.

(Just around the corner from here – first right along Canning Street – is the flat occupied for a time by John's art college friend and 'fifth Beatle', Stuart Sutcliffe.)

NO.7 PERCY STREET STU SUTCLIFFE'S FLAT

Here in the rear of the ground floor of No 7 was the 'artist's garret' occupied by Stu Sutcliffe, the Beatles' first base player. With his James Dean-like persona, he epitomised the romantic image of 'the sensitive artist'. He was regarded by his tutor Arthur Ballard, who gave him personal tuition here, as 'brilliant'

(Return to the junction of Canning Street and Hope Street, cross Hope Street and turn right.)

FORMER LIVERPOOL COLLEGE OF ART
(now part of Liverpool John Moores University) Hope Street
JOHN & STU SUTCLIFFE'S ART COLLEGE

Clutching a portfolio of his work from Quarry Bank High School and wearing his dead Uncle George's sports jacket and a collar and tie specially for the occasion, John scraped through the interview and was accepted as a student here in the Summer of 1957.

The college was a big disappointment to the idealistic seventeen year old Lennon. He was immediately strapped into the straightjacket of the lettering class with its overriding requirement for neatness and precision. John loathed it. It was totally alien to his restless, free-roaming spirit.

The only tutor to be remotely on the same wavelength as John was Arthur Ballard who observed: "He draws naturally. As a conventional art student he was not very good but as an artist, which is very much more important, he was very talented."

John himself later said of the three years he spent here: "All I ever learned in art school was about Van Gogh and stuff. They didn't teach me anything about Marcel Duchamp which I despised them for."

It was here that he struck up a close friendship with the very talented Stuart Sutcliffe and met his future wife Cynthia Powell. Polite and twin set prim, she must have appeared an unlikely partner for the disruptive and aggressive 'teddy boy' Lennon with his drainpipe trousers, long drape jacket, sideburns and D.A. (duck's arse) hairstyle.

At an end of term college party, Lennon sounded her out for a date. Awkwardly, Cynthia explained: "I'm awfully sorry, but I'm engaged to this fellow in Hoylake." to which Lennon acidly retorted: "I didn't ask you to marry me did I?" However, she did accept an invitation to join him and his mates for a drink in "Ye Cracke". After the drinking session they went back to Stu Sutcliffe's flat and made love. From then on their infatuation was mutual. They became inseparable. Their relationship was to end in acrimony in 1968 following John's affair with the Japanese artist Yoko Ono. He had first met Yoko in November 1966 at a private preview of her avante-garde art exhibition at London's Indica Gallery.

Sometimes an angel, more often a devil, his years at art college were difficult ones. As John later admitted: "I was in a sort of blind rage for two years. I was either drunk or fighting...There was something the matter with me."

The archetypal 'angry young man' both amused and appalled his fellow students with his grim humour mostly aimed at disabled or old people. "Some people will do anything to get out of the army." he'd shout after cripples. Cruel drawings showed women cooing "Aren't they lovely." over babies with horribly contorted faces. On the day the Pope died a Lennon cartoon showed him locked outside the gates of Heaven with the caption – "But I'm the Pope I tell you!"

In the basement was the college canteen, arched and dimly lit and reminiscent of the Cavern. Here, on the stage at the back, John, Cyn and Stu, joined by Paul and George with fish and chips from the local 'chippy', would gather for lunch and practice sessions.

Some of the embryo Beatles' earliest gigs were played here in the hall during Saturday night college dances. When they set off for Hamburg, they 'borrowed' the college's amplifier!

On a snowy 24 January 1984, Yoko brought Sean on a 'pilgrimage' to Liverpool to see some of his father's old haunts. They called here and generously presented the college with a complete set of John's Bag One lithographs. Rather embarrassingly, the valuable gift was later stolen from the college library. Their trip echoed an earlier pilgrimage Yoko and John had made to Liverpool in 1970. It was to be his last visit to the city.

Class of '56. The Liverpool Institute's Lower School, April 1956 (part 1)

Mike McCartney, Paul's   Paul McCartney
younger brother

FORMER LIVERPOOL INSTITUTE *Mount Street* –
PAUL & GEORGE'S HIGH SCHOOL
NOW LIVERPOOL INSTITUTE FOR PERFORMING ART (LIPA)

Founded in 1825, the Liverpool Institute, or the 'Innie' as it was known, was the city's top high school for boys. It was every Liverpool mother's dream that her son would pass the eleven-plus examination and win one of the prized places here even though he would immediately be branded a 'college pudding' by his lesser talented and no doubt envious mates.

The Innie's two most famous sons were Paul and George. Academically they were poles apart. Paul had already been here a year when George started in 1954; the Innie was to be their school until they left for Hamburg in 1960. Disinterested and rebellious from the start, George frittered away his opportunities and failed all his exams. He made a mockery of his school uniform by wearing tight drainpipe trousers and, once, a canary yellow waistcoat under his black school blazer. Not for George the regulation 'short back and sides' haircut. He grew his hair as long as he could, piled high in the Elvis and Tony Curtis styles of the day and topped by the universally hated school cap.

Whilst by no means an enthusiastic scholar, Paul was a natural student with the knack of being able to listen to the radio and do his school homework at the same time. He did just enough to get a respectable five GCE 'O' level and one 'A' level passes, failing in History, Geography, Scripture and German. One of his old maths

Neil Aspinall, the Beatles' Road Manger, was sometimes referred to as 'The Fifth Beatle'. He is now Apple's M.D.

Len Garry, bass player with the Quarry Men

Don Andrew & the late Colin Manley, bass player and lead guitarist, respectively, of the Remo Four

books from Class 4B, filled with doodles and scribbles, fetched £23,000 at a Tokyo auction in 1997.

The Institute had one big compensation for Paul and George. It was next door to the Art College, venue for practice sessions with John Lennon and Stu Sutcliffe.

After years of abandonment the Institute was given a new lease of life when Paul announced plans to convert it into a 'School of Fame' or, to give it its full and proper title 'The Liverpool Institute for Performing Arts' – 'LIPA' for short. "The initial reason for my involvement with LIPA was the building. It was my old school. When I saw for myself the state it had reached as an abandoned building, I wanted to save it." From drawing board to official opening took six years, the process being kicked off by a £1 million pound personal donation from Paul. This was followed by the pennies of Liverpool schoolchildren and the millions of pounds of sponsorship ploughed in by Grundig. Even the Queen and celebrities such as Eddie Murphy, Jane Fonda, Ralph Lauren and David Hockney contributed towards the £12 million cost of the venture.

The first 200 hundred students, chosen from applications that flooded in from around the world, started their three-year degree courses in January 1996. Towards the end of that first month, Paul McCartney, watched by Beatles record producer, George Martin, and Chief Executive, Mark Featherstone Witty, officially inaugurated LIPA by cutting a giant cake in the shape of his old school. On the same occasion,

Class of '56. The Liverpool Institute's Lower School, April 1956 (part 2)

The late Ivan Vaughan, John's boyhood friend and one-time member of the Quarry Men

(Top) Peter Sissons BBC Television Newsreader (Below) Alan 'Dusty' Durband, Paul's English master and former Chairman of the Everyman Theatre

Paul's old school assembly hall (now a 450-seat working theatre) was named the Paul McCartney Auditorium. But the real icing on the cake came when the Queen officially opened LIPA in May 1996. And when Paul was knighted he made his acceptance speech here.

Paul continues his active involvement with LIPA, attending its graduation ceremonies and making surprise visits to give masterclasses to its students.

(Continue along Hope Street. The next street on the left is Rice Street.)

Former Liverpool College of Art and its next door neighbour the Liverpool Institute, now LIPA.

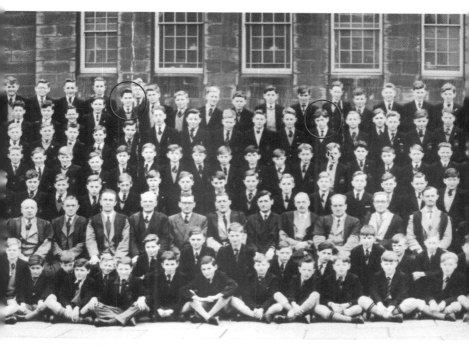

George Harrison

Les Chadwick of Gerry and the Pacemakers

'YE CRACKE' *Rice Street*

The local pub for students from the nearby Art College and, occasionally, mature looking schoolboys from the Liverpool Institute. 'Black Velvets' would be drunk by John, Stuart Sutcliffe and their other student cronies in boisterous lunchtime drinking sessions. His romance with fellow art student Cynthia Powell from posh 'over the water' Hoylake on the Wirral also blossomed here.

Frequently, they would be joined by their lecturer and ally, Arthur Ballard, who even conducted tutorials in the back room of the pub. John, who had recently lost his mother in an horrific road accident, drowned his sorrows here and often returned to the Art College in a drunken state. He later admitted: "When I went to art college in Liverpool, you know, it was mainly one long drinking session."

Drinking on one occasion was temporarily abandoned when the then-famous Liverpool-born film star John Gregson appeared outside the pub. Lennon, in typically unconventional fashion, managed to get his autograph...on a dirty old boot that was lying around! On another occasion John pretended to 'swim' in pools of beer on the bar room floor!

Drinking in this tiny pub, then as now, is very much an elbow to elbow affair.

(Almost opposite Percy Street is Falkner Street. With its cobblestones and old fashioned street lamps, you can easily imagine what this part of Liverpool looked like in Georgian times. Small wonder that the street is frequently used as a period piece film set.)

NO 36 FALKNER STREET
JOHN AND CYNTHIA'S HONEYMOON FLAT

The Beatles' manager Brian Epstein rented, but hardly ever used, the ground floor flat of this house. When John and Cynthia got married in August 1962, Brian let them honeymoon at the flat until they found a place of their own. Eventually, John and Cyn moved back to his Aunt Mimi's house in Menlove Avenue.

Whilst living here John had written *Do you want to know a secret?*, sung by George on the *Please, Please Me* album. It was also the song which had propelled another of Epstein's Merseybeat groups, Billy J Kramer and the Dakotas, to the top of the charts. John recalled the time he wrote the song:

"I was in the first apartment I'd ever had that wasn't shared by fourteen other students – gals and guys at art school. I'd just married Cyn and Brian Epstein gave us his secret little apartment that he kept in Liverpool for his sexual liaisons separate from his home life. And he let Cyn and I have that apartment."

(Re-trace your steps to Hope Street and to the right you will see the city's main classical concert venue, the Philharmonic Hall. Externally quite an attractive building, its art-deco interior is magnificent.)

PHILHARMONIC HALL *Hope Street*

In common with most Liverpool school-children, John, Paul, George and Ringo no doubt attended at least one concert at the 'Phil' by the RLPO (Royal Liverpool Philharmonic Orchestra) during the 50's.

From the late 50's it became a popular venue for pop groups, but not the Beatles. One of their early major influences, Buddy Holly and the Crickets, played here in 1958. The copyright to Holly's music is now owned by his biggest fan, Paul McCartney.

The by-now famous George was here again in 1963 as a panelist judging the final of the Lancashire and Cheshire Beat Group Competition. Also on the jury was Dick Rowe, forever remembered as 'the man who turned down the Beatles'. George had been impressed by a new R & B group he'd seen in London and suggested that Rowe should sign them up. The band?...the Rolling Stones. This time Rowe does the right thing and takes George's advice.

From time to time the hall echoes to orchestral versions of Beatle classics, most notably when their recording manager George Martin, sometimes dubbed 'The Fifth Beatle', conducted the orchestra. I have always thought it curious that their music was recorded by Arthur Feidler and the Boston Pops and not the RLPO with George Martin wielding the baton.

To celebrate the orchestra's 150th anniversary in 1991, Paul McCartney wrote a full-length orchestral symphony *Liverpool Oratorio* in collaboration with American-born composer Carl Davies. Although rehearsals took place here, the premiere was staged in the Anglican Cathedral on the 28th and 29th June. Fittingly, after being performed in twenty countries, the 100th performance took place here in September 1996 with the proud McCartney in attendance.

A pun on his 'working class' Liverpool roots, *Working Classical*, Paul's third orchestral work (the second was *Standing Stone*), performed by the London Symphony Orchestra with the Loma Mar Quartet, was premiered here on 16 October 1999. Paul and members of his family were in the audience. At around the same time, and in stark contrast to his late interest in orchestral and chamber music, Paul released *Run Devil Run*, comprised mainly of cover versions of rock and roll classics which influenced him as a teenager growing up in Liverpool in the 50's.

(From here look to the left and you will see another 'Phil' – the Philharmonic pub. To the right, look along Myrtle Street to the new building on the bend of the road.)

FORMER ROYAL LIVERPOOL CHILDREN'S HOSPITAL *Myrtle Street*
Demolished and replaced by Liverpool Community College's Arts Centre

When he was nearly seven years old Ringo was rushed here with violent stomach pains. His appendix had burst. Peritonitis set in and he slipped into a dangerous coma. He was not expected to survive that first night. Happily, he pulled through but recovery was slow and he remained here for about six months. Dogged by bad luck, he even managed to fall out of bed and injure himself just when he was about to return to his home in the nearby Dingle.

Illness struck Ringo down yet again when he was thirteen, this time with pleurisy. He was to spend another six months or so in the hospital's sanatorium (now demolished) at Heswall on the Wirral coast. It was there that he caught another bug...drumming.

His childhood friend and close neighbour Marie Maguire (now Marie Crawford and an official BeatleGuide) was a regular visitor to Heswall and remembers him as an enthusiastic member of the ward band. On one occasion she presented a delighted Ringo with Eric Delaney's record *Bedtime For Drums*. It was Marie who had taught the sickly Ringo, or 'Richy' as he was known to everyone in those days, to read and write. Illness had robbed him of even a basic education.

Now you see it, now you don't. The old Children's Hospital has been replaced by an Arts Centre.

The 'Phil' has been described as "The most decorative pub in Britain". The Roman Catholic Cathedral stands at one end of Hope Street, the Anglican Cathedral at the other.

PHILHARMONIC PUB *Hope Street*

This, the best example of Victorian pub exuberance in a city full of fine pubs, was frequented by the Beatles as an alternative to their regular pub 'Ye Cracke' a short distance further along Hope Street. John later bemoaned the fact that the price of fame was…"not being able to go to the Phil for a drink".

The 'Phil' is perhaps unique in allowing ladies to be given guided tours of the richly-marbled gents lavatories.

(Cross at the traffic lights and continue along Hope Street to the traffic lights.)

EVERYMAN THEATRE *Hope Street*

Although Merseybeat groups started to appear from late 1962, the Beatles never played here. However, it is known that George and Ringo came along to at least one of the poetry readings that were a feature of Liverpool's famous poetry scene in the 60's. "Liverpool is the centre of all human consciousness" – declared American guru Alan Ginsburg at the time. Liverpudlians loved him for it even though they didn't have a clue what he was talking about. Nor did they understand Carl Gustav Jung, the celebrated Swiss philosopher, when he pronounced, following a dream that changed his life, that "Liverpool is the Pool of Life."

The Everyman's real Beatle pedigree is to be found in the plays premiered here.

The Liverpool actor Mark McGann played the part of John in the Everyman's hit production of the play 'Lennon'

John, Paul, George, Ringo and Bert by Liverpool playwright Willy Russell, of *Shirley Valentine, Educating Rita* and *Blood Brothers* fame, had its world premiere here in 1974. It played to capacity houses for six weeks before transferring to the West End of London and then, in 1982, off-Broadway, New York, where it received indifferent reviews.

This was followed in 1981 by the premiere of *Lennon*, a musical play devised and directed by Bob Eaton and *Sgt. Pepper's Magical Mystery Trip* premiered here in 1996.

(Straight ahead is the R. C. Cathedral. Turn right into Oxford Street. The next street along is Arrad Street. Keep to the left of the new building in the centre of the road and you will see the former Maternity Hospital, known to many older Liverpudlians as 'The Stork Hotel'. Closed in 1995, it has been converted into student accommodation and is part of an extensive 'Student Village'.)

FORMER MATERNITY HOSPITAL *Oxford Street*
JOHN LENNON'S BIRTHPLACE

Here, in the old main building, at 6.30pm on Wednesday, 9 October 1940, Liverpool's most famous son, John Winston Lennon, was born. No memorial plaque was erected over his bed; nobody can even remember which ward he was born in! His Aunt Mimi favoured the name John and Winston was no doubt chosen as a patriotic tribute to Britain's great wartime leader Winston Churchill who was that very day elected leader of the Conservative Party.

On Saturday 12 October this notice of John's birth appeared in the Liverpool Echo:

> LENNON-October 9, in hospital to JULIA (nee Stanley), wife of
> ALFRED LENNON, Merchant Navy (at sea), a son-9 Newcastle Road.

John's own zany account of his birth, written for the *Mersey Beat* newspaper, is more interesting – "I was bored on the 9 October 1940, when, I believe, the Nasties were still booming us, led by Madalf Heatlump (who only had one). Anyway they didn't get me..."

Most accounts of John's birth tell of Aunt Mimi dodging shrapnel as she ran through the bomb-torn streets of Liverpool to see the new baby, who had to be placed under the bed during the air raid. It's a nice, whimsical, oft-told tale... but a tall one for all that. Official war records confirm that the Luftwaffe gave Liverpool a miss that particular night.

(Retrace your steps and cross at the lights into Mount Pleasant. The R. C. Cathedral is on the opposite side of the road. It has no Beatle connections but it is a modern classic and should definitely be visited.)

ROMAN CATHOLIC CATHEDRAL *Mount Pleasant*

Visitors to the R.C.Cathedral, or the Metropolitan Cathedral of Christ the King to give it its full title, either like it or they don't. From the outside it's a controversial building, architecturally, but reserve your judgement till you've looked inside. Most critics are stunned into silence.

Completed in 1967, it is known to irreverent Liverpudlians as 'The Mersey Funnel', 'The Pope's Launching Pad' or 'Paddy's Wigwam' because of its shape and the City's large Irish Catholic population.

You'll also find a coffee shop and toilets here.

(Continue down Mount Pleasant to Rodney Street at the next set of traffic lights. The second property on the left across the street is the birthplace of Beatles' manager Brian Epstein.)

NO 4 RODNEY STREET
BRIAN EPSTEIN'S BIRTHPLACE

Elegantly Georgian, Rodney Street is Liverpool's equivalent of London's 'street of doctors', Harley Street. Number 4 was the home of James Maury. He was appointed as America's very first Consul by George Washington in 1780 and was U.S. Consul in Liverpool from 1790 to 1829. Of more interest to Beatle fans, it was once a private nursing home and the birthplace, on 19 September 1934, of Brian Samuel Epstein – pronounced 'Epsteen' but known to the Beatles and his other Merseybeat groups simply as 'Eppy'. To the staff of his NEMS records shops he was the more formal 'Mr Brian'.

His parents, Harry and Queenie, were prosperous middle-class Jews and were easily able to afford a live-in nanny for Brian at their very 'des res' (desirable residence) in the posh end of Queens Drive.

At the height of the Beatles' success a radio interviewer asked Brian – "Were you born in Liverpool?" He replied, "I would have said it was essential.", the clear inference being that he could not have steered the Beatles to fame and fortune had he not been a fellow Liverpudlian.

(Keeping to the left, continue down the hill to No. 64 Mount Pleasant.)

FORMER REGISTRY OFFICE *64 Mount Pleasant*
JOHN AND CYNTHIA'S WEDDING

On Thursday 23 August 1962 a strange little ceremony was performed in this former Georgian town house and Registry Office built in 1773. The participants were John, Paul, George, Brian Epstein and Cynthia and her brother and his wife. Ringo wasn't there. He'd only just joined the Beatles and hadn't been invited. The occasion? The marriage of Beatle John to his pregnant art school girlfriend Cynthia Powell. The brief ceremony was conducted to the ear-splitting accompaniment of a pneumatic drill operated by a workman in the building next door.

Afterwards, they had all sprinted down the hill in the pouring rain to queue in Reece's restaurant for the wedding breakfast. John spent his wedding night playing a gig with the Beatles in Chester! There was to be no proper honeymoon either. The Beatles' crowded diary of engagements wouldn't allow it. It was a marriage destined not to last very long. Six years later, on 8 November 1968, it ended in the divorce court following John's admitted adultery with the Japanese artist Yoko Ono.

In this same Registry Office 25 years earlier, on 3 December 1938, John's mother Julia, a cinema usherette, had married ship's steward Freddie Lennon. The next day Freddie sailed off to the West Indies. Julia saw little of him during their brief and stormy marriage and, by the time John was 18 months old, Freddie had left them both for good.

(Continue to the bottom of Mount Pleasant – Adelphi Hotel is on the right.)

BRITANNIA ADELPHI HOTEL *Ranelagh Place*

Built during the days when Liverpool was the country's premier port for transatlantic passengers, the Adelphi is the 'Grand Duchess' of Liverpool's hotels. It also provides the setting for the annual Beatles Convention held every August and attended by fans from all over the world.

The American conventions are bigger and slicker affairs but the Liverpool event has that extra special ingredient that can't be found anywhere else in the world – after all, it is held in the city of the Beatles!

Yoko and Sean stayed here in 1990 when they were in Liverpool for John's memorial concert at the Pier Head.

(Look across the street to Lewis's store opposite)

LEWIS'S STORE *Ranalegh Street*

The top floor of this department store was the unlikely setting for a Beatles performance at a staff 'Young Idea Dance' for the '527 Club' on 28 November 1962.

And, for a short time, Paul even worked as a 'second man' on one of the store's delivery vans.

John and Cynthia regularly met under the store's dramatic statue of a naked man arms reaching heavenward. This once-controversial figure (known to many Liverpudlians, for obvious reasons, as 'Dickie Lewis') represents 'Liverpool Resurgent' and was sculpted by Epstein – Jacob, not Brian!

(Cross in front of the Adelphi Hotel, continue along Lime Street and cross Skelhorne Street. From here look across the road to the Wetherspoons pub, formerly Blacklers store.)

FORMER BLACKLERS STORE *Great Charlotte Street*

In between leaving school and joining the Silver Beetles on their tour of Scotland with Johnny Gentle in 1960, George Harrison served a brief apprenticeship here as an electrician – "I got a job cleaning all the lights with a paint brush, all those tubes to keep clean, and at Christmas I kept the Grotto clean."

NEMS opened their first city centre branch in Great Charlotte Street in the late 1950's. Brian Epstein ran the record section with military precision and made such a success of it that his father was quickly encouraged to open another, bigger, store in Whitechapel.

(Continue along Lime Street to the entrance to the train station)

LIME STREET TRAIN STATION

"Oh Maggie Maggie May, they have taken her away and she'll never walk down Lime Street any more." sang John in the Beatles' version of the famous Liverpool folk song *Maggie May*. A place of many Beatle comings and goings in the late 50's and early 60's.

(Look across the road to the left where you will see the Royal Court Theatre, Roe Street. The Beatles never performed there but in November 1979 Wings played four nights on the run, the first gig being an exclusive free concert given by Paul for masters and pupils from his old school, the Liverpool Institute. Julian Lennon also performed here in 1989. Look to the right to what is arguably the best building in Liverpool, St George's Hall.)

ST. GEORGE'S HALL *Lime Street*

Built in 1842, St George's Hall is ranked as one of the finest Graeco-Roman style buildings in the world and is a fitting memorial to its 23 year old architect, Harvey Lonsdale Elmes.

On 13 May 1960 this was the setting for a wild Liverpool Arts Ball, organised by Allan Williams and based on the famous Chelsea Arts Ball. He commissioned the Beatles to design and make decorative floats – one was in the shape of a guitar – which were destined to be destroyed by the revellers during the course of the evening. The ball ended in chaos with the hall's outraged owners, Liverpool City Council, swearing "never again". But memories are short and they allowed the 1984 Beatles Convention to take place here, this time without incident.

On the Sunday following John's murder, tens of thousands of still-grieving fans held an emotional vigil on the plateau in front of the hall where, two decades earlier, along with Paul and George and fellow art student Stu Sutcliffe, he had struggled with their carnival floats.

This spectacular building is regularly open for public viewing.

(Continue along Lime Street)

EMPIRE THEATRE *Lime Street*

The City's biggest and most glamourous theatre where, on 9 June 1957, the Quarry Men competed against other local hopefuls for the chance to appear on Carroll 'Mr Star-Maker' Levis's TV show. They failed this audition but were more successful when, as Johnny and the Moondogs, they competed here three times in October 1959, winning a place in the final round of auditions in Manchester.

Two weeks later, with the prospect of fame and fortune within their sights, John, Paul and George came back to Lime Street on the train from Manchester with their tails between their legs. The auditions had run on late into the evening. They didn't have the money to stay in Manchester overnight so they had to come home before it was their turn to audition.

When they returned to play the Empire again on 28 October 1962 the Beatles had really made 'the big time' in the eyes of their Liverpool fans, even though they took second billing to Little Richard, Craig Douglas, Kenny Lynch, Sounds Incorporated and Jet Harris.

Over the next two years the Beatles were to appear here on another six occasions two of which were especially memorable. On the afternoon of 7 December 1963, they had given a special concert for 2,500 members of their Northern Area Fan Club and had taken part in the filming of Juke Box Jury to the added delight of those same fans. That evening, as the Beatles gave two concerts at the Odeon cinema round the corner from the Empire, 23 million television viewers saw the unique 'Juke Box Jury' panel of John, Paul, George and Ringo pass judgement on a batch of the latest record releases.

This un-retouched version of the photograph that appears on page 1, shows that the Beatles stood in the shower of their cramped dressing room at the Empire Theatre for this photograph.

The Beatles' 11th and final appearance at the Empire took place on 5 December 1965. Little did their adoring army of local fans realise that it was also to be the very last time their idols were to perform in Liverpool as a group. However, George was back on stage here in 1969 with Delaney & Bonnie, Paul played here in 1973 and again in 1975 with his band Wings. And Ringo with his All Starr Band, featuring son Zak also on drums, was here in 1992.

(Turn right into London Road. On the next block is the Odeon cinema.)

ODEON CINEMA *London Road*

Before it was split into a number of smaller cinemas, the Odeon was one enormous 'picture palace'. On 7 December 1963 it was the venue for two performances by the Beatles following a hectic afternoon at the nearby Empire Theatre.

On 10 July 1964, the same day that the Beatles had been honoured at a civic reception at Liverpool Town Hall, the Odeon became the setting for the northern premiere of the Beatles' first film *A Hard Day's Night*. It was a Hollywood-style event easily surpassing the film's earlier Royal premiere in London. The 1969 film, *The Magic Christian*, in which Ringo co-starred with Peter Sellers, was also given its northern premiere here.

Another glittering event took place here on the evening of 28 November 1984 when Paul and Linda McCartney attended the UK premiere of Paul's film *Give My Regards To Broad Street*. During the afternoon Paul had been made an Honorary Freeman of the City of Liverpool.

Backbeat, which told the story of the Beatles' early days, was given its world premiere here on 24 March 1994.

CASSANOVA CLUB/PEPPERMINT LOUNGE *London Road/Fraser Street*

The Cassanova Club transferred to Sampson and Barlow's ballroom above the shops here from its short-lived home in The Temple, Dale Street, and was opened by local promoter Sam Leach on 9 February 1961. Two days later the Beatles played the first of seven dates here.

The following week, on Valentine's night, fans paid four shillings and sixpence (about 22 pence – refreshments included!) to bop to the Beatles, the Big Three, Rory Storm and the Hurricanes and Mark Peters and the Cyclones. The Cassanova Club hit the headlines 35 years later when the first-ever film footage of the Beatles – half a minute of colour film without sound, shot in the club on that very night – came to light.

Later, as the Peppermint Lounge, or 'The Pep' as it was known, it continued to be a popular venue for local groups although by then the Beatles had moved on.

Further down Fraser Street was Mr Pickwick's club, the setting for the first-ever Liverpool Beatles Convention on 8/9 October 1977, masterminded by Cavern DJ Bob Wooler and Beatles' 'manager' Allan Williams.

(Return to Lime Street and cross at the traffic lights into William Brown Street.)

Paul kindly loaned his precious drumskin for this part-reconstruction of Peter Blake's famous Sgt Pepper album cover. Fellow College of Art student, Ann Mason, contributed this unusual life study of John who normally avoided being seen with his hated, but necessary, spectacles.

WALKER ART GALLERY *William Brown Street*

One of Stuart Sutcliffe's paintings was selected from amongst thousands of entries for the prestigious bi-annual John Moores Liverpool Exhibition held here in 1959. Moores, founder of the Littlewoods football pools, catalogue and High Street stores empire, and after whom the city's newest university, the Liverpool John Moores University is named, bought the painting for £65 for his private collection. For the struggling art student it was in those days a princely sum. Stu promptly spent part of it on a down-payment for an electric base guitar enabling him to take his proper place in the Beatles' line up.

When he was 21 Stu died of a brain haemorrhage in the arms of his German fiance Astrid Kirchherr. He had been studying under Eduardo Paolozzi at the Hamburg College of Art. Two years later, in 1964, with Beatlemania at its height, his mother persuaded the Walker to stage an exhibition of his work. It ran from 2 to 24 May and was seen by over 11,000 visitors.

One of Stu's paintings, *'Hamburg Painting No.2'*, is owned by the Walker and is normally on view.

In 1983 I was asked to come up with ideas for how places like the Walker Art Gallery could celebrate Liverpool's International Garden Festival Year and generally make themselves more interesting to visit in 1984. Thus was born the concept of 'The Art of The Beatles' exhibition. Fellow Beatle project collaborator Mike Evans and I put together an exhibition which was sniffily accepted by the Gallery. It ran from May to September 1984, attracted nearly 50,000 paying visitors and was judged a great success. The fans certainly loved it!

Cynthia Lennon accepted our invitation to open the exhibition and related the times when she and John, as awestruck art students, would tip toe round the Walker speaking in whispers. He would have seen the funny side of 'The Art of The Beatles' show. By the Walker's standards, it was slightly irreverent – there was non-stop Beatle music and videos, a pile of bricks from the old Cavern (shades of the Tate!) and the hallowed walls displayed his once-banned 'Bag One' drawings alongside paintings from his childhood.

The exhibition later toured Japan and was also staged in Cologne.

(Next door to the Walker is the Picton Library.)

The Picton Library and its next door neighbour the Walker Art Gallery are in the heart of the 'Cultural Quarter'.

PICTON LIBRARY *William Brown Street*
PAUL'S 'FREEDOM OF THE CITY' CEREMONY

Lamentably, any proposal to honour Liverpool's most famous sons created discord in the city of their birth: 'twas ever thus. Nevertheless, on 7 March 1984, Liverpool City Council managed to pass a resolution bestowing on each Beatle the Honorary Freedom of the City, the highest honour it is possible for an individual to receive from the City. Passing a resolution was one thing. Getting the Beatles to come to Liverpool to be formally made Freemen of the City was something else. Yoko finally collected John's Freedom of the City award in a tree-planting ceremony in New York's Strawberry Field in October 1998. The City Council is still waiting to hear from George and Ringo!

Always the most amenable and public relations conscious of the Fab Four, Paul readily accepted the invitation. And it was in this impressive circular domed library that, on 28 November 1984, Paul McCartney MBE received the Scroll which confirmed his new status as a Freeman of the City.

At that time the infamous Militant-controlled Council was steering the City towards bankruptcy. "Does this mean I get to see the books?" Paul joked as he responded to speeches by Council worthies.

If the library is open pop in and have a look. It's very impressive.

(Cross St John's Gardens by the path at the rear of St George's Hall. This will bring you to the Swallow Hotel and the Tourist Information Centre.)

QUEEN SQUARE CENTRE

This is the city's main Tourist Information Centre, very useful for up-to-the-minute information about Liverpool, including any Beatle happenings that might be taking place. You'll also find a selection of Beatle souvenirs, postcards and posters, mostly relating to the city's association with the group.

You can also buy tickets for the 'Magical Mystery Tour' conducted by a guide in a coach which departs from a point nearby. It is also possible to book your own BeatleGuide for a personal tour of Fab Four haunts. A few of the guides knew the Beatles and have interesting first-hand stories to tell.

The helpful staff are always pleased to find accommodation for visitors to the city and to generally make sure that they make the most of their stay.

Merseyside

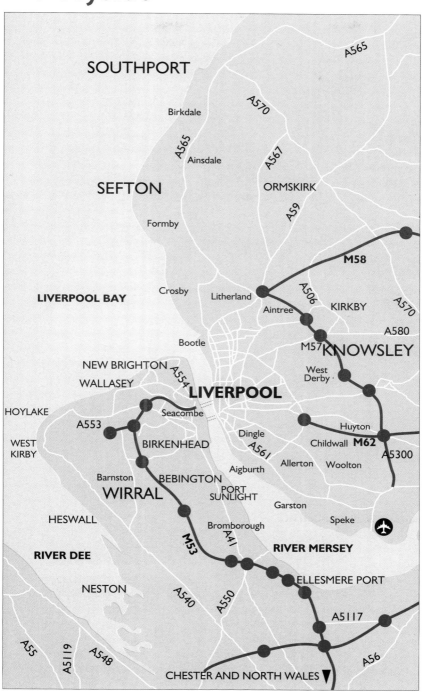

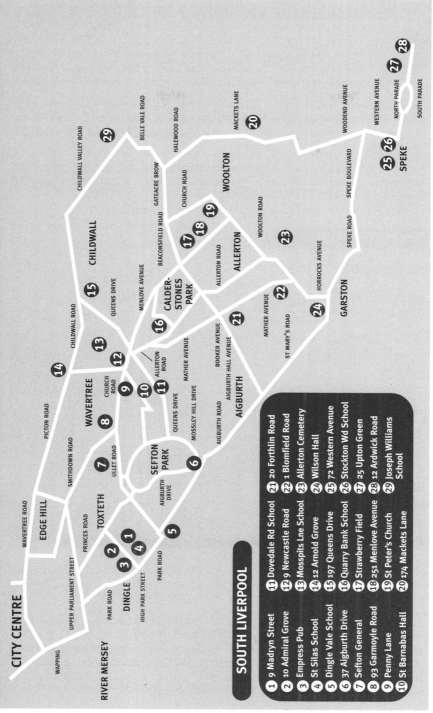

CITY CENTRE

WAPPING
WAVERTREE ROAD
EDGE HILL
UPPER PARLIAMENT STREET
PRINCES ROAD
PICTON ROAD
SMITHDOWN ROAD
RIVER MERSEY
TOXTETH
DINGLE
Park Road
HIGH PARK STREET
PARK ROAD
AIGBURTH DRIVE
ULLET ROAD
CHILDWALL VALLEY ROAD
BELLE VALE ROAD
HALEWOOD ROAD
CHILDWALL ROAD
CHILDWALL
WAVERTREE
CHURCH ROAD
MENLOVE AVENUE
QUEENS DRIVE
GATEACRE BROW
BEACONSFIELD ROAD
CHURCH ROAD
WOOLTON
WOOLTON ROAD
ALLERTON
ALLERTON ROAD
CALDER-STONES PARK
SEFTON PARK
MOSSLEY HILL DRIVE
QUEENS DRIVE
ALLERTON ROAD
MATHER AVENUE
BOOKER AVENUE
AIGBURTH HALL AVENUE
AIGBURTH ROAD
AIGBURTH
MATHER AVENUE
ST MARY'S ROAD
HORROCKS AVENUE
GARSTON
SPEKE ROAD
SPEKE BOULEVARD
WOODEND AVENUE
WESTERN AVENUE
NORTH PARADE
SOUTH PARADE
MACKETS LANE
SPEKE

SOUTH LIVERPOOL

1 9 Madryn Street
2 10 Admiral Grove
3 Empress Pub
4 St Silas School
5 Dingle Vale School
6 37 Aigburth Drive
7 Sefton General
8 93 Garmoyle Road
9 Penny Lane
10 St Barnabas Hall

11 Dovedale Rd School
12 9 Newcastle Road
13 Mosspits Lne School
14 12 Arnold Grove
15 197 Queens Drive
16 Quarry Bank School
17 Strawberry Field
18 251 Menlove Avenue
19 St Peter's Church
20 174 Mackets Lane

21 20 Forthlin Road
22 1 Blomfield Road
23 Allerton Cemetery
24 Wilson Hall
25 72 Western Avenue
26 Stockton Wd School
27 25 Upton Green
28 12 Ardwick Road
29 Joseph Williams School

(Opposite page) The time: Saturday, 16th July 1957. The place: St Peter's Church, Woolton. The occasion: the church's Summer fete when the 16-year old John Lennon met the 15-year old Paul McCartney for the first time.

47

Here is a selection of some of the more important Beatle places outside the city centre but still within or near the Liverpool boundary. For ease, I've grouped them under South Liverpool and North & East Liverpool.

The number after each of the addresses indicates the postal districts into which the city is divided. However, to help you find your way around the city, I suggest you buy a good street map, available from most bookshops, many newsagents or the city's two Tourist Information Centres.

All the places can be reached by public transport; for information, 'phone the Merseytravel Line on 0150 236 7676 seven days a week 8am to 8pm or visit the Queen Square or Paradise Street Travel Centres.

SOUTH LIVERPOOL:

'RINGOLAND' – The Dingle

NO 9 MADRYN STREET *off High Park Street, Dingle, Liverpool 8*
RINGO'S BIRTHPLACE

Humble birthplace of the eldest Beatle. Richard ('Richy') Starkey, alias Ringo Starr, was born in the front room of this Victorian terraced house on 7 July 1940, a month before Hitler started his bombing raids on the nearby docks.

Ringo was just three when his mother Elsie and father, also Richard, split up. Elsie worked as a part-time barmaid to make ends meet, leaving young Ringo either with neighbours or more often than not with Grandma and Grandad Starkey who lived at the end of the street at No 59 (pictured above). Grandad Starkey, a boilerman who worked at the docks, once made Ringo a big train 'with real fire in it' which not surprisingly was the talk of the street. Fitting then that much later in life Ringo should be so closely associated with the popular 'Thomas the Tank Engine' stories for which he did the voice-over.

Partly because the rent was cheaper, partly to avoid bumping into her ex-husband who was also living in Madryn Street, but mainly to help an old friend who had a husband and three children, Elsie swapped her house for her friend's even smaller 'two up, two down' house in nearby Admiral Grove when Ringo was six years old.

After many years of dereliction and abandonment, Ringo's birthplace was sold at a Tokyo auction in March 1997 for £13,250. The house has since been renovated.

NO.10 ADMIRAL GROVE
off High Park Street, Liverpool 8
RINGO'S HOUSE

Cool dude. Ringo photographed in the nearby docklands shortly after joining the Beatles.

Ringo's tiny 'two up, two down' home from the age of six until fame and fortune beyond his wildest imaginings were heaped on his humble shoulders after just six months as the Beatles' new drummer. Ever since, it seems to me, Ringo has had that permanent "How did all these wonderful things happen to an 'ordinary' little boy from Liverpool like me?" look about him!

Ringo's mother re-married in April 1954 when he was nearly 14. Her new husband, whom she had known for many years, was a Londoner called Harry Graves. After the war and an illness, he had come to Liverpool to take up a place on a Government training scheme for painters and decorators and, amazingly, 'for a

beneficial change of air'! Remember, in those pre-Clean Air Act days, Liverpool had a well-deserved reputation for being one of the most air-polluted and soot-blackened cities in Britain, a place where lung-searing smogs were common.

The irony was compounded that same year when Ringo caught a cold which developed into pleurisy and affected his lungs. He was sent to convalesce at the Children's Hospital at Heswall on the healthy Wirral coast. He remained there for six months...but he was the drummer in the ward band!

Ringo pictured in the Cavern soon after joining the Beatles in August 1962. The famous Beatles' 'dropped T' logo did not appear on his drum kit until the following year.

To Elsie's joy, Ringo and Harry hit it off from the start. Unwittingly, it was Harry who probably sparked off Ringo's fascination for all things American including a thwarted teenage attempt to emigrate to Texas. Harry was a painter at the giant United States Air Force base at Burtonwood near Liverpool and he often brought home the genuine American 'DC' comics, film magazines, candy and gum much prized by Liverpool children who usually had to make do with inferior English substitutes. He was also a very good singer and the 'star turn' at family parties.

When he left school at 15 having missed so much of his education through illness, Ringo became, in rapid succession, a British Rail messenger boy, a steward on the cruise boat 'St.Tudno' that once sailed between Liverpool and Llandudno and an apprentice fitter with H. Hunt and Son, Speke. Also at Hunts was his next door neighbour Ed Myles. During the skiffle craze Ringo joined his Eddie Clayton skiffle group, later to become the Clayton Squares.

When he was 20, and by then drummer with the hugely popular Merseybeat group Rory Storm and the Hurricanes, Ringo packed in his apprenticeship at Hunts and set off with the band to enter the 'big time'... a 13 week season at Butlins Holiday Camp in Pwllheli, North Wales! It was here that he first became known as Ringo Starr and even had his own 'Starr-Time' solo spot with the group.

The following Summer, Ringo celebrated his 21st birthday with a party at 10 Admiral Grove. Difficult though it is to believe, about 60 people crammed into this tiny house, including Cilla Black, Gerry and the Pacemakers and the Big Three.

On 30th August 1963 all four Beatles were here for the filming of footage for the documentary 'The Mersey Sound'. John and Paul took a back seat on this occasion whilst Ringo was filmed emerging through the front door, fighting his way past hordes of small kids and getting into George's open-top car.

Elsie and Harry clung onto their home in the Dingle until 1965 when fan fever became just too much. However, unlike the other Beatle parents, they insisted on staying in Liverpool so Ringo bought them a luxurious bungalow in Woolton, a select area of the city, where they spent their remaining years.

THE EMPRESS PUBLIC HOUSE
High Park Street, Liverpool 8

To Beatle fans who own Ringo's first solo album 'Sentimental Journey', this typical Liverpool street corner pub will look familiar. He used a photograph of it on the front cover; the people in the windows are members of his family. The back cover features the former grocer's shop on the corner of Kinmel Street (opposite The Empress).

ST. SILAS CHURCH OF ENGLAND PRIMARY SCHOOL
Pengwern Street, Liverpool 8
RINGO'S FIRST SCHOOL

Ringo was just five years old when he began his primary school education here. He got off to an inauspicious start. On his very first day he came home at mid-day and told his mother that he didn't have to go back that day. She believed him...until she spotted all the other kids returning to school!

When he was almost seven his education suffered a serious setback. An attack of appendicitis worsened into peritonitis with the result that he spent a year away from school. Luckily, he had a close childhood friend, Marie Maguire, who helped him to catch up. Now Marie Crawford she is, appropriately, an official BeatleGuide as well as Godmother to Zak, Ringo and Maureen's first child.

Brian was best man at Ringo and Maureen's wedding at London's Caxton Hall on 11th February 1965. The marriage ended in divorce ten years later. Maureen died of leukaemia in 1994.

DINGLE VALE SECONDARY MODERN *(now Shorefields)*
Dingle Vale, Liverpool, 8
RINGO'S SECONDARY SCHOOL

Ringo's school, from the ages of 11 to 15, although the final two years were again spent in hospital or at home. Not surprisingly, he left without any qualifications.

When he approached the school for an end-of-school report for use as a reference in his search for a job, he claimed that it was so long since he'd last been there that nobody could remember him. Ironically, when Ringo hit the big time, the school dragged out 'his' desk at one of their open days and charged visitors for the privilege of sitting in it!

SEFTON PARK

NO.37 AIGBURTH DRIVE *Sefton Park, Liverpool 17*
STUART SUTCLIFFE'S HOME, NOW BLENHEIM LODGE

Empty and derelict for many years, Stu's house was transformed into this hotel in 1991. Sefton Park's most prominent structure, the Victorian Palm House, was similarly derelict but has been rescued, partly with the help of a donation from George Harrison.

Stu Sutcliffe, who preceded Paul McCartney as the Beatles' bass player, lived in this handsome Victorian villa overlooking Sefton Park boating lake. He was born in Edinburgh on 23 June 1940 but the Sutcliffe family subsequently moved to Liverpool. He was already showing great artistic promise as a student at the Liverpool College of Art when he left here to move into a flat at 7 Percy Street near the college.

After his second trip to Hamburg with the Beatles, Stu decided to stay there with his German photographer girlfriend, Astrid Kerchherr, and study under Eduardo Paolozzi at the State Art College in the city. The following year, on 10 April 1962, he died of a cerebral haemorrhage in Astrid's arms as an ambulance sped them to hospital.

SEFTON GENERAL HOSPITAL *Smithdown Road, Liverpool 15*
JULIAN LENNON'S BIRTHPLACE

Apart from the sign at the entrance, very little remains of this hospital, birthplace, on Monday 8 April 1963, of John Charles Julian Lennon – John after his famous father, Charles after Cynthia's father and Julian, the nearest they could get to John's mother Julia.

The umbilical cord had been coiled around Julian's neck and when he made his grand entrance he was, to quote his mother, 'an awful yellow colour'. John missed all the drama; he was on tour in the South of England at the time. Two days later he was back on Merseyside playing the Majestic Ballroom in Birkenhead and saw his new son for the first time.

"Who's going to be a famous little rocker like his dad then?", John would ask the gurgling infant cradled in his arms. His visits to see Julian and Cynthia created enormous interest among staff and patients eager to catch a glimpse of the by now famous Beatle father.

But this hospital held bittersweet memories for John. Five years earlier he had rushed here by taxi to be given the devastating news that his beloved mother Julia had died following a road accident. Coincidentally, Julia's common law husband, John Dykins, also died here after being involved in a traffic accident in 1969. Their two daughters, John's half-sisters Julia and Jacqui, were also born here.

93 GARMOYLE ROAD
off Smithdown Road, Liverpool 15
CYNTHIA LENNON'S FLAT

Cynthia and Paul's girlfriend, Dot, both rented adjacent rooms in this house for a short time in 1962. It has two claims to fame. Paul McCartney, who had bought engagement rings for Dot and himself, ended their relationship abruptly here one night. And Julian Lennon was conceived here. When Cynthia broke the news of her pregnancy to John he was horrified but, as was the fashion in those days, he readily agreed to 'do the right thing'…"There's only one thing for it, Cyn, we'll have to get married."

PENNY LANE AREA

PENNY LANE Liverpool 18

Here it is! The street made famous in the Beatles' evergreen song 'Penny Lane'. The shelter in the middle of the roundabout, the barber shop, the bank…they are all here, sometimes even beneath blue suburban skies.

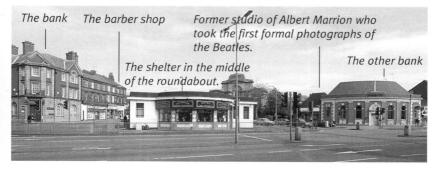

The bank   The barber shop   Former studio of Albert Marrion who took the first formal photographs of the Beatles.

The shelter in the middle of the roundabout.

The other bank

If you stand here long enough, you may see the banker who never wears a mac or even the pretty nurse selling poppies from a tray. However, you will probably stand a better chance of seeing a fireman with his clean machine; perhaps he'll even have an hourglass and a picture of the Queen. The local fire station is only a short distance away.

John explained that when he wrote this song with Paul he was re-living his childhood. He lived in Newcastle Road, just around the corner from Penny Lane, for the first five years of his life. Daily for another six years he walked down Penny Lane to and from school. As a mischievous schoolboy he rode on the bumpers of the tramcars and did some petty thieving from the shops in Penny Lane. Later, with his group the Quarry Men, he played gigs at St Barnabas Church Hall in Penny Lane. Penny Lane was very much 'in his eyes and in his ears'.

An exasperated Liverpool City Council long ago gave up replacing the heavy metal Penny Lane name signs removed by souvenir hunters. Now the name is simply painted on the wall. In spite of this, strangers often have difficulty finding this street, the narrowest of six roads that all come together at what Liverpudlians call 'the Penny Lane roundabout'.

As an art student, Cynthia whiled away the summer holidays serving behind the cosmetics counter of Woolworths store here. On one occasion when she was shopping in Penny Lane she was gripped by labour pains...Julian Lennon was about to make his entrance into the world.

At St.Barnabas Church on 29 May 1982, Paul's brother Mike, formerly Mike McGear of The Scaffold, married the lovely Rowena Horne. Paul, who had once been a choirboy at St.Barnabas, was the best man.

The 'shelter in the middle of the roundabout' is now the home of Sgt.Pepper's cafe, a convenient watering hole for Beatle fans.

ST. BARNABAS CHURCH HALL
Penny Lane, Liverpool 18

The Quarry Men played here as an interval skiffle group at a number of Saturday night dances in the late 50's. Although St.Barnabas Church is situated at the 'Penny Lane Roundabout', this one-time church hall, now called Dovedale Towers and no longer connected with the church, is half way down the road.

Opposite is the Penny Lane 'Chippy' ("Penny Lane is in my eyes, a four of fish and finger pies") and the Penny Lane Cake Shop whose next door neighbour is Messrs Strange and Strange...very strange!

John when he was a seven year old pupil at Dovedale.

DOVEDALE ROAD *off Penny Lane, Liverpool 18*
JOHN AND GEORGE'S INFANT AND JUNIOR SCHOOL

John first enrolled at Dovedale Road Infants School here on 6 May 1946. The 'Literary Lennon' quickly emerged and soon he was reading and writing fluently. Although he was inspired by books such as *Alice in Wonderland*, *Wind in the Willows* and *Just William*, John was an original thinker – "He won't do anything stereotyped" said his Headmaster. Even at that early age John himself recognised that somehow he was 'different' from the other kids.

He was just seven when he wrote his first 'book' – *Sport, Speed and Illustrated*. It saw the emergence of his distinctive style of jokes, drawings and stories alongside pasted-in images of film stars and footballers. Indeed, the sleeve of John's *Walls and Bridges* album features paintings of footballers and Red Indians done by him in his final term here in June 1952 when he was 11 years old.

Although he didn't know it at the time, there was another younger little boy with latent special talents at Dovedale at the same time as John. His name was George Harrison. John transferred to the Junior Boys School here in 1948 and finally left Dovedale for Quarry Bank Grammar School after he'd passed his '11-plus' exam in 1952. A few years later, George passed the same examination and joined Paul at the Liverpool Institute.

George and John, Dovedale's most famous 'old boys'.

9 NEWCASTLE ROAD *Liverpool 15*
JOHN'S FIRST HOME

Just around the corner from Penny Lane, this is the house where John was conceived and where he lived from the time he was a few days old until he was about five. Then he moved a few miles away to 'Mendips' to continue being cared for by his Aunt Mimi and Uncle George.

This was the home of the Stanley family. John's mother, Julia, was a tall, vivacious red head and the youngest of George ('Pop') and Annie Stanley's five daughters. She was also spirited, fun-loving and unconventional.

She married Freddie Lennon, a ship's waiter in the Merchant Navy, on the 3rd December 1938. They spent their 'honeymoon' at the Trocodero Cinema in London Road. At the end of the film Julia returned here and Freddie went back to his lodgings, sailing off the next day on a three-month trip to the West Indies. When John was 18 months old, Freddie left him and Julia for good. Shortly afterwards, unable to cope, Julia had virtually 'given' John to her sister Mary (Mimi) to raise.

A wartime affair with a soldier resulted in another baby which she immediately arranged to have adopted. After the war, Julia lived here with her new man, John 'Bobby' Dykins (John nicknamed him 'Twitchy') whom she'd met whilst working for a time as a waitress at a cafe in Penny Lane. They and their daughter, also Julia, moved to 1 Blomfield Road in 1949, the year that their second daughter, Jacqueline, was born.

WAVERTREE

MOSSPITS LANE INFANTS SCHOOL
Mosspits Lane, Liverpool 15
JOHN'S FIRST SCHOOL

Contrary to what is stated in virtually all the Beatle and Lennon books, this, not Dovedale Road Primary School, was the very first school attended by John. He enrolled here on 12 November 1945 and the school's Admission Book shows his address as 9 Newcastle Road and his parent/guardian as his father Alfred. John remained here for no longer than 6 months since, by 6 May 1946, he had moved to Dovedale Road Infants School.

12 ARNOLD GROVE *Wavertree, Liverpool 15*
GEORGE'S BIRTHPLACE

Birthplace on 25 February 1943 of the youngest Beatle, George Harrison. He lived in this cramped 'two up, two down' house with an outside lavatory (rent 50p a week) for nearly seven years with his sister Louise, brothers Harold and Peter and mother and father, Louise and Harold.

When George was five he enrolled at Dovedale Road Primary School. His elder brother Peter was already there, in the same class as John Lennon.

George's mother and father, a bus driver and former steward on White Star liners sailing from the Pier Head, had been on the housing waiting list for 18 years when they finally got the news that they'd been allocated a brand new Council house in Speke. They packed up all their belongings and left here the day after New Year's Day 1950.

197 QUEEN'S DRIVE
Liverpool 18
BRIAN EPSTEIN'S HOUSE

This is the comfortable home in one of the city's more affluent suburbs into which Brian Epstein was born in 1934. His parents, Harry and Queenie, had moved into their new five-bedroomed detached house shortly after they married a year previously.

11-year old Brian (right) with Mother Queenie and brother Clive in the garden of 197 Queens Drive.

The Epstein family had run a furniture store in Liverpool's Walton Road since the beginning of the century. When he left school in 1950, virtually an academic failure, Brian reluctantly joined the family business. Although he had set his heart on becoming an actor, and had even studied for a time at the Royal Academy of Dramatic Art (RADA), it was not to be. Eventually, he channelled his energy and artistic talent into the family furniture and record stores with remarkable success.

To mark Paul's 21st birthday on 18 June 1963, Brian and his family hosted a morning cocktail party in the lounge of this house. Later that same day at another party held for Paul at his Aunty Jin's house at 147 Dinas Lane, Huyton, John beat up Cavern DJ Bob Wooler for insinuating that he was having a homosexual affair with Brian.

John, who lived not too far away from here, was a regular visitor, sitting with Brian in the morning room as they planned the Beatles' career.

QUARRY BANK *(Now Calderstones School)* Harthill Road, Liverpool 18
JOHN'S GRAMMAR SCHOOL

Almost from that day in September 1952 when he first entered the Tudor-style Quarry Bank, formerly a mansion built by a local timber merchant, John was to be the bane of his teachers' lives and the despair of his Aunt Mimi. End of term school reports provide the clue – "Hopeless. Rather a clown in class. A shocking report. He is just wasting other pupils' time. Certainly on the road to failure."

His best subject was class anarchy of which he was the undisputed leader. Fighting, smoking 'loosies' (cigarettes bought in one's and two's by those who couldn't afford a full packet), disrupting classes, canings, refusing to conform and even being banned from school were the tarnished hallmarks of an undistinguished five-year academic career at Quarry Bank. He left on 24 July 1957 after failing all his O Level examinations, even in his favourite subject, art.

Paradoxically, his Quarry Bank days were creatively, if not academically, productive. School exercise books were filled with highly original and devastatingly funny stories, poems, drawings and cartoons. One called *The Daily Howl* which mercilessly parodied his teachers was passed under the desks from one giggling schoolboy to the next. A weather report read – 'Tomorrow will be Muggy followed by Tuggy, Wuggy and Thuggy.' A cartoon showed a blind man with glasses leading a blind dog, also with glasses. The physically afflicted were frequently the butt of his humour. This early work was to form the basis for his acclaimed books *In His Own Write* and *A Spaniard in the Works*.

It was also at Quarry Bank that John formed his first band, the aptly named Quarry Men, who were in essence a skiffle group made up of his classroom cronies. For his parting shot, John had fronted the Quarry Men at the end of term school dance held here in July 1957. Goodbye Quarry Bank, hello Liverpool College of Art and the bohemian life of an art student!

Left: Standing on John's right is blond-haired Pete Shotton, boyhood friend and fellow Quarry Man. Right: William Ernest Pobjoy, Headmaster of Quarry Bank during John's final year. Like his predecessor, he failed to 'knock him into shape' but John gave him gave him credit for getting him into art college.

STRAWBERRY FIELD *Beaconsfield Road, Liverpool 25*

A short distance up the hill on the right hand side, look out for the old sandstone gate pillars inscribed 'Strawberry Field', the ornate strawberry coloured gates and the closed-off pathway leading to...'Strawberry Fields Forever'. Just stand there quietly and soak up the atmosphere of the place that inspired John Lennon to write his haunting masterpiece of pop imagery.

Major British artist Maurice Cockrill's interpretation of Strawberry Field.

Opened as a Salvation Army Children's Home in 1936, Strawberry Field was a large Victorian mansion set in extensive grounds. It was demolished in the late 60's and the land at the rear sold off to help pay for the newer buildings you see today.

Often as a young boy, John would come here with his Aunt Mimi to join in the fun of the Summer Fete. It clearly held a special place in his heart. His association with Strawberry Field is a long one and continues to this day. He made a donation to the appeal for the new annexe, named Lennon Court when it opened in 1979. As part of their Liverpool 'pilgrimage', Yoko and Sean visited Strawberry Field in January, 1984, to meet the staff and children.

On 9th October that year, John's birthday, a parcel arrived from Yoko. It contained a cheque for $90,000, three records, a photograph and a poem specially written by Yoko. She still keeps in touch with Strawberry Field.

Through a gift of $1m from Yoko, a 'twin' Strawberry Fields was created in 1985 out of a neglected tear-shaped section of Central Park, New York (entrance by the Women's Gate at West 72nd and Central Park West). John and Yoko lived nearby in the Dakota Building. On the 9th October 1998 Yoko and the Lord Mayor of Liverpool planted an oak tree there in John's honour. Yoko also collected the Freedom of the City of Liverpool scroll awarded posthumously to John in 1984. Coincidentally, Britain's first public park, at Birkenhead on Merseyside, was used as the model by the great American parks pioneer Frederick Olmstead to create New York's Central Park.

(Strawberry Field is still a Salvation Army Children's Home and under no circumstances whatsoever should you enter the grounds.)

'MENDIPS' 251 MENLOVE AVENUE *Liverpool 25*
JOHN'S HOUSE

As this neat semi-detached suburban home testifies, and contrary to media mythology, John Lennon, the 'Working Class Hero' who never did a day's manual labour in his life, did not come from the slums of Liverpool.

The Second World War had just ended when John came to 'Mendips' to be brought up by his Aunt Mimi and her dairy farmer husband, George. It was to be John's home until Beatle fame forced him to move to London in 1963. He spent more time here than anywhere else in his 40-year life.

It was here that he had been smitten by the rock and roll bug after hearing Elvis's 'Heartbreak Hotel' on Radio Luxembourg. If the charismatic, swivel-hipped Presley ignited the spark, it was the decidedly un-hip British skiffle singer Lonnie Donegan who fanned the flame.

The whole appeal of skiffle, based on three simple guitar chords, was that it was so easy, anybody could do it. John was no exception. From the time that he carefully unwrapped his first £5 "guaranteed not to split" mail order guitar, the die was cast. From then right up to his death in 1980 he was to be a rock and roll musician.

Man and boy: cover of John's 'Menlove Avenue' album and John, five, around the time he moved to 'Mendips'

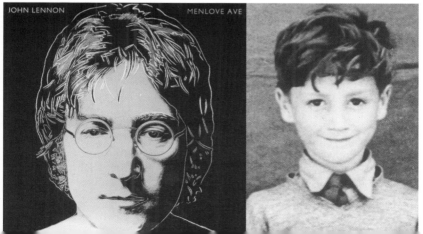

Left: Yoko and Sean visited 'Mendips' when they came to Liverpool in 1984. Centre: John's bedroom was over the front porch. Right: John aged seven standing outside the front porch of 'Mendips'.

Soon John was writing songs of his own. *The One After 909* was one early effort written whilst still at school. Other early songs written by John here in 'Mendips' include *I Call Your Name*, *Hello Little Girl* and *Please, Please Me*. John wrote this in his bedroom over the front porch. Just before his death he was to recall the exact day, even remembering the colour of the coverlet on his bed and Roy Orbison's *Only the Lonely* which, along with Bing Crosby's *Please, lend your little ears to my pleas*' inspired him to write *Please, Please Me*, the first of an unbroken chain of twelve No.1 hits for the Beatles.

His loving but authoritarian Aunt Mimi did not encourage his new-found love affair with the guitar and regularly banished him and the peace-shattering instrument out of earshot to the glazed front porch with the scolding – "The guitar's all very well John, but you'll never make a living out of it." John later had these immortal words framed and they took pride of place in Mimi's bungalow overlooking Poole Harbour in Dorset. John bought her this luxury home in 1965 when the attentions of the growing army of fans laying siege to 'Mendips' in the hope of a sighting of the famous Beatle became too much to take. She lived there until her death on 6 December 1991.

Today, all that remains are the memories. But just look at 'Mendips'...and 'Imagine': The carefree childhood days John spent here with Mimi, his doting uncle George, his three cats, Titch, Tim and Sam and the family mongrel dog Sally. The frequent visits from his 'real' mother, Julia, vivacious, carefree and a kindred free spirit. Imagine John, the rebellious teenager cycling to Quarry Bank School followed by tormented art student days as the archetypal 'angry young man'. And, later, John the family man living here with his wife Cynthia and new son Julian.

Imagine too, Paul, George and Pete Best knocking on the front door to join John in early Beatles rehearsals – with Mimi well out of the way, of course! And visits from their new manager, Brian Epstein. Imagine also the times John returned to 'Mendips' drained from long nights in the seedy clubs of Hamburg, sweat-sodden from the cellar clubs of Liverpool and light-headed from tours carried along on waves of Beatlemania. Imagine it all.

And best of all, Imagine, just Imagine as, guitar in hand, Lennon the uncompromising genius sat on the edge of his bed or stood in this porch creating and singing some of those classic songs for which the Beatles will forever be popular.

In 1999 English Heritage decided that John's Liverpool home should be marked with a Blue Plaque.

MENLOVE AVENUE
THE DEATH OF A MOTHER

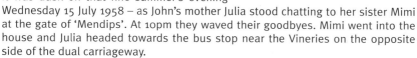

It was dusk on that fine summer's evening – Wednesday 15 July 1958 – as John's mother Julia stood chatting to her sister Mimi at the gate of 'Mendips'. At 10pm they waved their goodbyes. Mimi went into the house and Julia headed towards the bus stop near the Vineries on the opposite side of the dual carriageway.

As she stepped from the grassed central reservation into the second carriageway of Menlove Avenue she did not see the grey Standard Vanguard saloon car, registration number LKF 630, driven by off-duty Police Constable 126 Clague, bearing down on her in the half-light.

Minutes later John's schoolfriend Nigel Whalley hammered on Mimi's door to deliver the grim news that her sister had been involved in an accident. Mimi dashed across to where Julia lay unconscious in a pool of blood. Near the bus stop, a distance of 58 feet further back up the road, her bag and its contents poignantly marked the spot where she had been sent spinning through the air. Quickly, Mimi returned to 'Mendips' for her coat and climbed into the ambulance which sped them through the Penny Lane roundabout and on to Sefton General Hospital.

Julia was pronounced 'dead on arrival'. The autopsy report noted a large fracture at the base of her skull and other injuries.

Accounts of the tragedy were wildly contradictory. Constable Clague claimed that he had been travelling at well under 30 miles per hour, that Julia had walked into his path, that he had sounded his horn and had braked, that he had even mounted the central reservation, missing trees in the process, in a desperate bid to avoid hitting her. Two eye witnesses, a 15 year old shipping clerk and a man riding his bicycle in the same direction, told a completely different story. They both said the car was going very fast, that it did not sound its horn and that the brake lights did not come on.

The inquest, exactly one month after the accident, recorded a verdict of 'misadventure'. Constable Clague later stood trial but was acquitted.

For John, the 17 year old art student who had recently 're-discovered' the mother he had 'lost' as a child, this second loss – for good this time – was almost more than he could bear. Externally, it was expressed in heavy drinking and the aggressive and often cruel 'hard man' front that he presented to the world. Internally, his sensitive feelings were later to find an outlet in songs such as *Julia* and the heart-rending *Mother*.

ST. PETER'S CHURCH *Church Road, Woolton, Liverpool 25*
JOHN MEETS PAUL FOR THE FIRST TIME – 'WHERE IT ALL BEGAN'

Just imagine. 16-year old John Lennon is fronting his skiffle group, the Quarry Men. In the audience is 15-year old Paul McCartney. It is the first time in his life he has clapped eyes on John but it was a moment he would never forget - "I remember when we first met, at Woolton, at the village fete. It was a beautiful summer day and I walked in there and saw you on stage. And you were singing 'Come Go With Me' by the Del Vikings. But you didn't know the words so you made them up..." (Photo by Quarry Man, Geoff Rhind)

This is the unlikely setting for the historic first meeting of the 20th century's two most famous singer/songwriters. On Saturday, 6th July 1957, the 15 year old Paul McCartney, wearing his flash white sport coat and black drainpipe trousers, cycled from his home in Allerton to St. Peter's. He'd come at the suggestion of Ivan Vaughan, a class-mate, to see the Quarry Men, a skiffle group for which Ivan sometimes played tea chest bass. And, there might also be the chance of chatting up some girls.

The grave of Eleanor Rigby (pictured right) is directly opposite St Peter's Church Hall – shown in the background in this photograph.

That afternoon, in a field behind the church, John Lennon and his Quarry Men Skiffle Group sang their way through skiffle standards like *Railroad Bill*, *Cumberland Gap* and *Maggie May*, as well as rockers such as *Be Bop A Lula* and hits of the day like the Dell Vikings's *Come Go With Me*. Paul was mightily impressed even though John had stumbled over the words of every song and had to improvise.

Afterwards, in the church hall across the road where the Quarry Men had been booked to play an evening gig, he was introduced to the group by Ivan Vaughan. Paul showed them how he played *Twenty Flight Rock*, *Be Bop a Lula* and other songs from his repertoire. Not only did Paul know all the words but he could play proper chords *and* tune a guitar, a skill that had thus far evaded John Lennon.

Paul later recalled their first meeting…"I remember this beery old man getting nearer and breathing down me neck as I was playing. 'What's this old drunk doing?' I thought. Then he said *Twenty Flight Rock* was one of his favourites. So I knew he was a connoisseur. It was John. He'd just had a few beers. He was 16 and I was only 14 (just 15 actually), so he was a big man". "I remember him in a checked shirt with slightly curly hair and I thought: He looks good – I wouldn't mind being in a group with him." Years later, John was to say "That was the day, the day I met Paul that it started moving."

Although John had more or less decided that day that he wanted him in the Quarry Men, it was a week or so before the message was finally passed to Paul – "D'ya wanna join me group?" And it wasn't until 18 October that Paul eventually made his debut with the Quarry Men.

On the 40th anniversary of John and Paul's first encounter a weekend of special celebrations was held here. There was a garden fete, a memorabilia sale, John's original band, 'The Quarry Men', reformed and played a gig and a commemorative plaque was unveiled at the end of a special church service at St Peter's. The Queen, Prime Minister, John's two wives and Paul were amongst the many who sent personal messages.

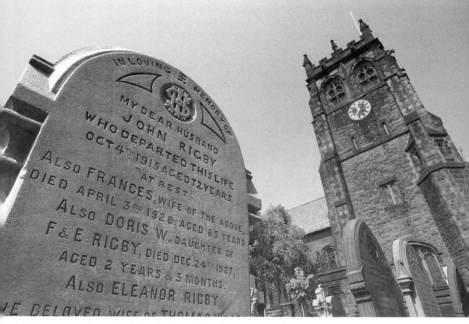

John Lennon attended St Peter's Sunday School when he was a young boy. As he played in the old churchyard could he have seen the name 'Eleanor Rigby' on this gravestone and stored it away in his sub-conscious? And remember that John met Paul for the very first time just yards away from here so is there a possibility that Paul might have seen it too? See also page 88.

174 MACKETS LANE
Hunts Cross, Liverpool 25
GEORGE'S HOUSE

The Harrison family lived here between 1962 and 1965 during which time George and the Beatles soared to worldwide fame.

Like the other Beatle houses in the 60's this Council house became the focal point for George's fans. Fan mail by the sackload was delivered and often the fans themselves turned up on the doorstep in the hope of a 'sighting'. Finally, in 1965, George's father quit his bus driver's job and the Harrisons moved into a house bought for them by George near Warrington.

1 BLOMFIELD ROAD *Liverpool 19*
JULIA LENNON'S HOUSE

Unbeknown to John for a number of years, this is the house where his real mother Julia lived. It is less than two miles away from where he lived with her sister, his Aunt Mimi, who to all intents and purposes had been his mother since he was a toddler.

The 1940's had been a turbulent period for Julia. It was wartime. She'd had a baby, John, been deserted by her sailor husband Freddie, 'given' John away to her sister to be brought up and had another wartime baby by a soldier. This child, Victoria, was born in the 'Elmswood' Nursing Home, North Mossley Hill Road, Liverpool, in June 1945 and had immediately been adopted by a Norwegian and taken to Norway.

After the war Julia had formed a steady relationship with John 'Bobby' Dykins, a head waiter in a Liverpool hotel, and had two daughters, Julia and Jacqueline, by him. It was a relationship that was to last for the rest of her life, even though it was never formalised by marriage; Julia never got round to divorcing Freddie Lennon.

During John's teenage years 1 Blomfield Road virtually became his second home. These were the years when he 're-discovered' his mother, although she was more like an older sister or fellow conspirator than a real mother. She was naturally musical and could play the piano and banjo and even juggle! Like John, she was a big Presley fan and even had a stray cat called Elvis.

Here, Julia taught John his first chords on a cheap 'guaranteed not to split' guitar; albeit they were banjo chords! Best of all, she never objected to John and his Quarry Men using her home for rehearsals. The bathroom, where the sound of guitar and washboard would bounce off the hard tiles, was a favourite bolthole for the young musicians.

John frequently stayed here, sometimes for days at a time. During one occasion, on 15 July 1958, a policeman knocked on the door to tell him and Bobby that Julia had been involved in a traffic accident. They rushed in a taxi to Sefton General Hospital, Smithdown Road, only to be told the horrible truth – the happy-go-lucky Julia, a woman in her prime, was dead. For the devastated seventeen year old John, this was the second time in his young life that he'd 'lost' his mother, this time for good.

ALLERTON CEMETERY *Allerton Road, Liverpool 19*
JULIA'S GRAVE

This is the final resting place of Julia Lennon. She was buried here in Church of England Section 38, grave No.805, at 10am on Monday, 21 July 1958. She was 44 years of age. The grave, which is unmarked, is a private one and Julia is the only member of the family buried there.

20 FORTHLIN ROAD *Allerton, Liverpool 18*
PAUL'S HOUSE
(Now owned by the National Trust)

The McCartney family had moved house many times over the years but it was definitely a step up in the world when, in 1955, they moved from the tough Speke housing estate to Forthlin Road in the genteel leafy suburb of Allerton.

Mrs McCartney was delighted with her new home and was over the moon when her two sons won places to the Liverpool Institute, arguably the best grammar school in the city. Her joy was to be very short-lived. Along came 'Maxwell with his silver hammer' and she died of breast cancer after a short illness on 31st October 1956, leaving husband Jim to bring up Paul and his younger brother Mike. Mary's grave can be found in Yew Tree Cemetery, Section 3A, Grave 276. Tragically, Paul's wife Linda was also to fall victim to breast cancer in 1998. With Paul's backing, the Linda McCartney Centre, which provides specialist treatment for breast and others cancers, was opened two years later at the Royal Liverpool University Hospital.

In this house Paul was to 'lose' himself in his guitar, even taking it to the bathroom where the excellent acoustics compensated for the lack of an amplifier. After Paul's historic first encounter with John Lennon at the Woolton Parish Church Garden Fete on 6 July 1957, this house became a favourite rehearsal venue for the newly-formed, but soon to be formidable, Lennon and McCartney song-writing partnership. They wrote about 20 songs here before their first single *Love Me Do* gave them chart success.

Unlike John's Aunt Mimi, Paul's dad was himself no mean musician and actively encouraged the boys. In any case he was at work all day in the Liverpool Cotton Exchange. And when the cat's away...and play they certainly did. Here, in the front room of this house, Paul and John would collaborate on the dozens of songs to be written down in school exercise books. At other times they would draw each other, raid the larder, bring girls back and even smoke Ty-Phoo tea-leaves in Jim's pipe!

After the Beatles returned from their triumphant American tour in 1964, Paul bought his dad 'Rembrandt', a very 'des res' in Baskervyle Road in posh Heswall on the Wirral. With a removal van ordered for midnight, the Macs avoided the attentions of fans, media and curious neighbours by doing a moonlight flit.

Because of its importance in the history of popular music, the National Trust bought this house when it came on the market in 1996. This was a 'first' for the Trust which is noted for rescuing great historic houses and grand country estates rather than humble suburban council houses. Much altered over the years, the house has been restored to what it looked like when Paul lived here. Visitors are treated to an exhibition of brother Mike's photographs of family life at Forthlin Road, an audio tour and a display of Beatles memorabilia. Tours by minibus start from Albert Dock or the Trust's Speke Hall, a magnificent half-timbered Tudor mansion near Liverpool Airport (*'phone 0151 708 8574 for tours information*)

SPEKE, GARSTON AND BELLE VALE

WILSON HALL *Speke Road, Garston, Liverpool 19*
GEORGE'S FIRST MEETING WITH JOHN AND THE QUARRY MEN

Re-built as a Lennon's supermarket (no relation!), and now the Woolton Carpet Centre, this was the site of Wilson Hall where the Quarry Men played four times to a largely local audience of Teddy boy roughnecks.

More significantly, it was here, on 6 February 1957, that an embryonic 14 year old teddy boy by the name of George Harrison first saw the Quarry Men and was introduced to their leader John Lennon.

72 WESTERN AVENUE *Speke, Liverpool 24*
PAUL'S HOUSE

The McCartneys moved to this new council housing estate from their flat in Sir Thomas White Gardens, Everton, when Paul was four. Among the tricks he and brother Mike got up to was to throw stones at their neighbour's tree 'to speed up the growth of the apples'!

Paul's mother, Mary, worked locally as a midwife whilst father Jim was a cotton salesman for the Liverpool firm of A. Hannay and Co. He was an accomplished musician and during his inter-war bachelor years had led Jim Mac's Band.

After the McCartney's got a transfer to a brand new Council house in nearby Ardwick Road, another midwife moved in with her family. Her daughter Shelagh, now Shelagh Johnston, is an official BeatleGuide and Manager of The Beatles Story, Albert Dock.

STOCKTON WOOD ROAD PRIMARY SCHOOL *Speke, Liverpool 24*
PAUL'S FIRST SCHOOL

A short walk from Paul's home in Western Avenue, this was his first school. The post-war 'baby boom' pushed the school population over the 1,500 saturation level making it the biggest infants school in England, at which stage Paul and his brother Mike were moved to the Joseph Williams Primary School in Gateacre.

12 ARDWICK ROAD *Speke, Liverpool 24*
PAUL'S HOUSE

After Western Avenue, the McCartneys moved to this new Council house before leaving the sprawling Speke Council estate for Forthlin Road in 1955. Living just around the corner from here in Upton Green was George who often travelled on the same bus as Paul to their school, the Liverpool Institute.

25 UPTON GREEN *Speke, Liverpool 24*
GEORGE'S HOUSE

The Harrison family had been on Liverpool Corporation's housing waiting list for 18 years when, the day after New Year's Day 1950, they at last moved to this new house. Compared with their tiny 'two up, two down' house in a back street cul-de-sac in Wavertree, this house must have seemed palatial. And there was a 'green' where children could play safely under the watchful eyes of their mothers.

George was six years old at the time and this was to be his home until 1 October 1962 when the family moved to Mackets Lane in Hunts Cross, a posher part of Liverpool. Luckily, George's mother positively approved of his struggle to master the guitar so this was always a favourite house for practice sessions.

At the nearby British Legion Club in Damwood Road the Rebels, featuring George and his brother Peter, played their one and only gig in 1956 for the princely sum of ten shillings (fifty pence) each.

Believe it or not but this house was also the highly unlikely setting for a Quarry Men gig – no doubt an unpaid one! The occasion? Big brother Harry's wedding reception on 20th December 1958.

JOSEPH WILLIAMS PRIMARY SCHOOL
Naylorsfield Drive, Belle Vale, Liverpool 25
PAUL'S SCHOOL

A half hour journey from Speke, this was Paul and brother Mike's school for a number of years before they both passed the 11-plus examination and moved on to the Liverpool Institute. Whilst at 'Joey' Williams, Paul went through his 'fat school-boy' period.

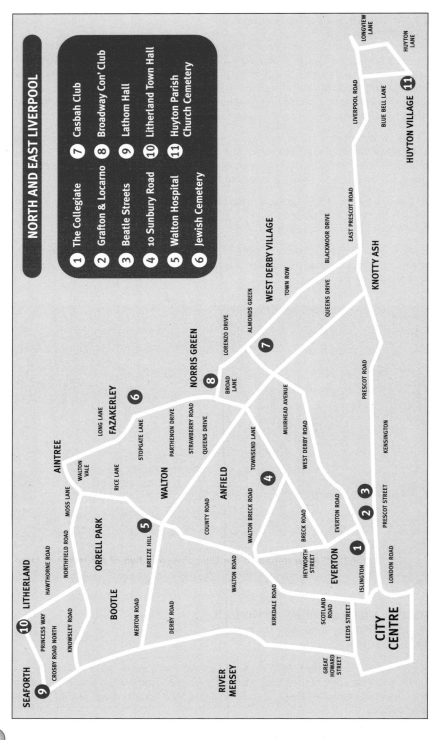

NORTH AND EAST LIVERPOOL

1. The Collegiate
2. Grafton & Locarno
3. Beatle Streets
4. 10 Sunbury Road
5. Walton Hospital
6. Jewish Cemetery
7. Casbah Club
8. Broadway Con' Club
9. Lathom Hall
10. Litherland Town Hall
11. Huyton Parish Church Cemetery

SEAFORTH
LITHERLAND
BOOTLE
ORRELL PARK
AINTREE
FAZAKERLEY
WALTON
ANFIELD
EVERTON
NORRIS GREEN
WEST DERBY VILLAGE
KNOTTY ASH
HUYTON VILLAGE
CITY CENTRE
RIVER MERSEY

CROSBY ROAD NORTH
PRINCESS WAY
HAWTHORNE ROAD
KNOWSLEY ROAD
NORTHFIELD ROAD
MOSS LANE
WALTON VALE
LONG LANE
RICE LANE
STOPGATE LANE
PARTHENON DRIVE
STRAWBERRY ROAD
QUEENS DRIVE
LORENZO DRIVE
ALMONDS GREEN
TOWN ROW
QUEENS DRIVE
BLACKMOOR DRIVE
EAST PRESCOT ROAD
LIVERPOOL ROAD
LONGVIEW LANE
HUYTON LANE
BLUE BELL LANE
PRESCOT ROAD
MUIRHEAD AVENUE
WEST DERBY ROAD
BROAD LANE
TOWNSEND LANE
WALTON BRECK ROAD
COUNTY ROAD
BRECK ROAD
EVERTON ROAD
HEYWORTH STREET
WALTON ROAD
MERTON ROAD
DERBY ROAD
BREEZE HILL
KIRKDALE ROAD
SCOTLAND ROAD
LEEDS STREET
GREAT HOWARD STREET
ISLINGTON
LONDON ROAD
PRESCOT STREET
KENSINGTON

FORMER COLLEGIATE *Shaw Street, Liverpool 6*
PETE BEST'S GRAMMAR SCHOOL

The Collegiate vied with the Liverpool Institute for the reputation of being the best grammar school in the city. Pete Best was a sixth form student here, leaving in 1958. The following year he met the frequently drummerless Quarry Men – John, Paul and George – and the year after that he finally joined the Beatles for their first trip to Hamburg. The Collegiate is being redeveloped for inner city living accommodation; happily the imposing original facade of the building has been retained.

THE GRAFTON AND THE LOCARNO BALLROOMS
West Derby Road, Liverpool 6

The 'Gravvie', affectionately known for its 'Grab-a-granny' nights, and next door neighbour, the 'Loc' (now re-named the Olympia) were two of a number of large, popular 'palais de dance' venues on the fringe of the city centre where the Quarry Men and later the Beatles played during the late 50's and early 60's.

When the Beatles first performed at the 'Loc' on 14 February 1963 at a special St. Valentine's Night dance, they had already recorded their *Please, Please Me* album. They appeared four times at the 'Gravvie', their parting gig taking place on 2 August 1963. This was to be their final Merseyside dance hall date. The following night would see their last-ever appearance at the Cavern.

In 1983 Paul invited me to meet him on the set of *Give My Regards To Broad Street*. It was a big thrill to watch the filming of his terrific rocker *Ballroom Dancing*, no doubt inspired by the likes of the 'Gravvie' and the 'Loc'.

'BEATLE STREETS' *Kensington Fields Estate, Liverpool 6*

After long and intensive campaigning by a small band of stalwart local Beatle fans, the Council reluctantly agreed to name four of the streets on this 1981 private housing estate after the Beatles. A number of owners have named their houses – look out for 'Imagine' and 'The Cavern'!

As well as John Lennon Drive, Paul McCartney Way, George Harrison Close and Ringo Starr Close, there are now Epstein Court, Apple Court and Cavern Court. Nearby, and coincidentally, you will find Sutcliffe Street, although this is an old Liverpool street.

10 SUNBURY ROAD *Anfield, Liverpool 4*
PAUL'S FIRST HOUSE

Jim and Mary McCartney moved into furnished rooms here after their wartime wedding in April 1941. It was to this house in June of the following year that the newly-born Paul was brought from Walton Hospital.

Soon, however, the McCartneys were on the move again, first to 92 Broadway, Wallasey, then to a pre-fabricated bungalow at Roach Avenue, Knowsley, on the outskirts of Liverpool. Then it was back to the city centre to a ground floor flat in Sir Thomas White Gardens, Everton, followed by a move to the giant new Speke estate and another two houses before the restless McCartneys settled in Forthlin Road, their last Liverpool home.

WALTON HOSPITAL *Rice Lane, Liverpool 9 (now part of Aintree Hospitals)*
PAUL'S BIRTHPLACE

Birthplace of Beatle Paul or, to give him his full name, James Paul McCartney. Paul's mother Mary had once been a sister on the maternity ward here and had qualified for a private ward for the birth of Paul, her first child, on 18 June 1942. Both of Paul's parents were in their thirties when they married – Jim was 39, Mary 32. Paul's brother Mike was also born here, on 7 January 1944.

Paul's birth certificate was sold at a Bonham's auction in Tokyo in March 1997 for a staggering £51,715. Paul was understandably miffed to put it mildly that, quite literally, his birthright had been 'stolen' from under him.

JEWISH CEMETERY *Long Lane, Aintree, Liverpool 9*
BRIAN EPSTEIN'S GRAVE

Following his tragic death at his London flat from an overdose of the drug Carbrital on 27 August 1967 at the age of 32, Brian Epstein's body was carried from Liverpool's Greenbank Drive Synagogue and buried here in Grave H12, Section A.

Along with the Epstein family at the graveside ceremony at 7pm on 29 August were Brian's favourites – Cilla Black, Gerry (of Gerry and the Pacemakers) and Nat Weiss, his American friend and lawyer. In defiance of the Jewish rule forbidding flowers at funerals, Weiss tossed a newspaper containing a single hidden white chrysanthemum onto Brian's coffin, a farewell request from George on behalf of the Beatles.

Brian's father, mother and brother are also buried here.

8 HAYMAN'S GREEN *West Derby, Liverpool 12*
PETE BEST'S HOUSE & CASBAH COFFEE CLUB

On 29 August 1959, as the Quarry Men, John, Paul and George performed at the opening night of this social club for teenagers created in the basement of Mona Best's rambling Victorian house. From then until June 1962 they played 44 gigs at the Casbah.

Mona's son had also been smitten by the rock and roll bug and played drums with his Blackjacks group. His name was Pete Best and by August 1960 he had joined the Beatles as their new drummer on their first trip to Hamburg.

Two years later, on 16 August 1962, to the fury of his many fans, he was unceremoniously dumped by the Beatles in favour of Ringo Starr. Too good looking? Not up to the mark as a drummer? Didn't fit in with the other Beatles? No convincing explanation has ever been given for this 'knife in the back' episode and to this day Pete Best is adamant that he still doesn't know why he was sacked. Suffice it to say that none of the Beatles had the guts to tell Pete to his face. They left the dirty work to Brian. Less than a month later they had recorded *Love Me Do* and were on their way to fame and fortune leaving behind a devastated Pete Best. Happily, Pete did not allow this crushing blow to embitter him for long.

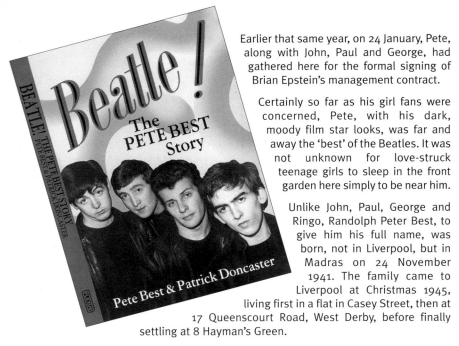

Earlier that same year, on 24 January, Pete, along with John, Paul and George, had gathered here for the formal signing of Brian Epstein's management contract.

Certainly so far as his girl fans were concerned, Pete, with his dark, moody film star looks, was far and away the 'best' of the Beatles. It was not unknown for love-struck teenage girls to sleep in the front garden here simply to be near him.

Unlike John, Paul, George and Ringo, Randolph Peter Best, to give him his full name, was born, not in Liverpool, but in Madras on 24 November 1941. The family came to Liverpool at Christmas 1945, living first in a flat in Casey Street, then at 17 Queenscourt Road, West Derby, before finally settling at 8 Hayman's Green.

Pete, a family man and retired Civil Servant, has made quite a few appearances as a guest speaker at Beatle Conventions. More interestingly, he has formed his own band and tours extensively. Royalties from *The Beatles Anthology*, where Pete's drumming is featured on ten tracks, has meant that some 35 years on Pete was finally able to reap the considerable financial rewards from recordings made during his days with the early Beatles.

To mark the 40th anniversary of the Casbah in 1999, local Merseybeat-era bands performed for fans in the grounds of this house. They were also able to see the ceilings covered in original Lennon and McCartney artwork and a portrait of George Harrison painted on a wall by Cynthia Lennon. A replica of part of the Casbah was installed in the Beatles Story museum at Albert Dock and plans were unveiled to re-open the Casbah Coffee Club for pre-booked tours.
Enquiries –
Tel: 0151 291 9764
www.casbahcoffeeclub.com

CLUBMOOR CONSERVATIVE MEN'S CLUB *Back Broadway, Liverpool 11*
PAUL'S FIRST GIG WITH JOHN AND THE QUARRY MEN

Previously, as the New Clubmoor Hall, this saw Paul's very first appearance with John and the Quarry Men, on 18 October 1957. It was an occasion memorable only because Paul, on his first and virtually last instrumental solo, fluffed '*Guitar Boogie*'.

LATHOM HALL *Lathom Avenue, Seaforth, Liverpool*

Once a cinema, this was yet another of the unprepossessing suburban 'jive halls' on the early Beatles circuit. It is notable for being the very first officially advertised gig for the 'Silver Beats' on 21 May 1960. However, it was one they never played since they were in Scotland on the final leg of the Johnny Gentle tour.

As the Silver Beats, they had played an interval spot the week previously and went on to play a few more engagements early in 1961. That first night base player Stu Sutcliffe had been roughed up in fight. John and Pete Best had gone to his rescue and John ended up with a broken finger. The oft-repeated story that Stu had been kicked in the head and that this resulted in his death from a brain haemorrhage two years later in Hamburg is, according to Pete Best who witnessed the incident, a myth.

LITHERLAND TOWN HALL *Hatton Hill Road, Litherland*
BIRTHPLACE OF "BEATLEMANIA"

Litherland Town Hall, prime contender for the title of the 'unlikeliest-looking Town Hall in England', hosted scores of Beatles gigs during 1961.

However, they had played here on one historic occasion in 1960. On 27 December, in a £6 booking arranged by Bob Wooler and billed as 'Direct from Hamburg', the Beatles brought the house down, invoking early scenes of the 'Beatlemania' that went on to sweep through the country and encircle the globe. Fame and fortune were now within their grasp.

The leather-jacketed Beatles had only played North Liverpool once before and many in the audience that night really did believe that they were a German group. Local promoter Brian Kelly knew when he was onto a good thing and immediately booked them for no less than 36 dances over the next three months. It was to establish them as Merseyside's top rock and roll band.

They played their final gig here on the evening of another historic day, 9 November 1961. As the Beatles were playing a lunchtime session at the Cavern that day, Brian Epstein came to see what all the fuss was about. As they say, the rest is history.

HUYTON PARISH CHURCH CEMETERY *Stanley Road/Blue Bell Lane, Huyton.* STU SUTCLIFFE'S GRAVE

Although Stu Sutcliffe died in Hamburg on 10 April 1962, he was not, contrary to popular belief, buried there. His final resting place is in this cemetery, grave number 552 in the 1939 section.

Visitors wanting to see the grave should make prior arrangements by telephoning 0151-449 3900

Bill Harry, Editor of Mersey Beat, presents the Beatles with their very first trophy, The Mersey Beat Popularity Poll shield, at Birkenhead's Majestic Ballroom.

BABY YOU CAN DRIVE MY CAR

BEATLE PLACES TO VISIT 'ACROSS THE WATER' IN WIRRAL

see map on page 83

WIRRAL

Wirral, the peninsula which lies between the River Mersey and the River Dee, is by far the most scenic of Merseyside's five 'boroughs'. Although the Mersey may seem like a barrier, two road tunnels, an underground railway, a ferryboat service and even a road and rail bridge at Runcorn, mean that travelling between Liverpool and Wirral is a breeze.

When Merseysiders want a day out on their doorstep, they head for either Wirral or Southport. When they were young the Beatles were no exception; favourite play-grounds for them were the New Brighton and Wallasey beaches.

Deceptively gentile, Wirral can lay claim to a number of Beatle 'firsts'. These include the very first time John, Paul, George and their new drummer, Ringo, performed on stage together, the first time they played in suits, the first booking organised for them by their new manager, Brian Epstein, and the first time they shared the bill with rock and roll superstars of their day such as Little Richard.

MAJESTIC BALLROOM *Conway Street, Birkenhead*

Latterly a bingo hall, this was once a large, prestigious venue operated by the Top Rank organisation and an important one for the Beatles. They made seventeen appearances here between June 1962 and April 1963, perhaps the most memorable being on 15 December when they were crowned 1962's undisputed 'Kings of Mersey Beat' at the first *Mersey Beat* poll awards show (see photograph opposite). Runners up were Lee Curtis and the All Stars...whose drummer was the recently deposed Pete Best.

GROSVENOR BALLROOM *Grosvenor Street, Liscard, Wallasey*

Another suburban dance hall that finally yielded, at least temporarily, under the onslaught of rock 'n' roll by the likes of Gerry and the Pacemakers and the Beatles who played here 14 times during 1960 and 1961. Memorable only because the gig on 10 March 1961 was the very last one booked for them by Allan 'The Man Who Gave Away The Beatles'/'The Man The Beatles Told to F... off' (take your pick!) Williams and for the punches which were often swung during its 'Swing Sessions'. In those days you could book the Beatles for about £10!

FORMER TOWER BALLROOM
Promenade, New Brighton

The Beatles played numerous gigs here between 1961 and 1963, most notably for Sam Leach's ambitious 'Operation Big Beat' shows which featured up to twelve acts on the one bill.

The highlight of the Beatles' many appearances here was undoubtedly on 12 October 1962, the week after '*Love Me Do*' had been released, when they were second on the bill to one of their all-time heroes, Little Richard. Embarrassingly, the recently-ousted Pete Best was also there that night – as drummer with Lee Curtis and the All Stars. On other occasions the Beatles shared the stage with Bruce Channel, Joe Brown & his Bruvvers and the Clan McLeod Pipe Band!

A spectacular fire in 1969 marked the end of the Tower Ballroom and Grounds which had once boasted a tower bigger than Blackpool's as well as a large fun fair.

HULME HALL *Port Sunlight Village*
'BIRTH OF THE BEATLES'

The unlikely but truly historic venue on 18 August 1962 for the real 'Birth of the Beatles'. This marked Ringo Starr's very first appearance as the Beatles' drummer. The Fab Four were complete. It was one of four gigs played in this Tudor-style village hall during 1962 for such hip bodies as the Horticultural Society, the Golf Club and the Recreations Association.

Don't leave this unique and beautiful village, created over a century ago by soap baron Lord Leverhulme, without visiting the 'jewel in the crown', the Lady Lever Art Gallery. It is truly exquisite and ranks among the world's top art museums so be prepared to be impressed.

The ante-room to the gentlemen's lavatory was the makeshift studio for this local hospital radio interview when the Beatles appeared at Hulme Hall on 27 October 1962. During the interview Paul confirms that John is indeed the leader of the group.

18 TRINITY ROAD *Hoylake*
CYNTHIA'S HOME

This was the Powell family's modest home where Cynthia was living when she and John Lennon met at the Liverpool College of Art and embarked on a passionate teenage love affair.

Once, following a vigorous love-making session in Stu Sutcliffe' flat, she ended up in the nearby Hoylake Cottage Hospital with grumbling appendicitis. She was visited by a concerned John, although for his first visit he brought George along too! Afterwards, John and George called here to tuck into plates of egg and chips served up by Cynthia's mother.

Here Cynthia also eagerly awaited the arrival of John's letters from Hamburg described by him as "The sexiest this side of Henry Miller. Forty pages long some of them".

In between leaving 'Mendips' and finally moving to London, this was 'home' for Cynthia, Julian and John, although he was almost constantly on the road at this time. During this period John took Cynthia on a belated Parisian honeymoon. Soon after they returned, the Press discovered that they were married and laid siege to the house in the hope of a sighting of the famous Beatle with his new wife and baby Julian.

MACDONA HALL *Banks Road/Salisbury Avenue, West Kirby*

After coming under his wing one week earlier, this was the first real booking the Beatles' new manager Brian Epstein arranged for them. The date was 1 February 1962 and Brian, in true showman style, had advertised it as the 'Grand Opening of The Beatle Club'. In fact, this was the only time they played here and nothing more was heard of The Beatle Club!

The gig took place in the hall used as a dance studio above the restaurant which, in those days, was occupied by the Thistle Cafe.

BARNSTON WOMEN'S INSTITUTE *Barnston Road, Heswall*

The Beatles were booked by the Heswall Jazz Club to play three dates in this village hall in 1962. Their first appearance, on 24 March, was something of a red letter day; they wore their new stage suits for the very first time. The grey suits were specially made by master tailor Beno Dorn following a visit to his shop in Birkenhead by the Beatles and Brian Epstein.

'REMBRANDT' *Baskervyle Road, Heswall*

Overlooking the Dee estuary and the hills of North Wales, this is the house which Paul bought for his father for £8,750 when he returned from America after the Beatles' triumphant tour of America in 1964. Compared with their small terraced house in Forthlin Road, this five bedroomed detached house was truly palatial.

Crippled by arthritis, Jim McCartney eventually moved to a bungalow nearby and died in March 1976. 'Rembrandt' was bought from his father by Paul and is still owned by him.

Wirral

THE BEATLES PLAYED HERE!

MERSEYSIDE VENUES PLAYED BY THE BEATLES/QUARRY MEN

LIVERPOOL CITY CENTRE:

Cabaret Club *28 Duke Street*

Cassanova Club
The Temple, Temple Street

Cassanova Club *1st floor ballroom,
corner London Rd/Fraser St*

The Cavern *10a Mathew Street*

David Lewis Club *Great George Place*

Empire Theatre *Lime Street*

Iron Door Club/Liverpool Jazz Society
13 Temple Street

Jacaranda Coffee Bar *23 Slater Street*

Lewis's Department Store
Ranelagh Street

Liverpool College of Art *Hope Street*

Merseyside Civil Service Club
Lower Castle Street

Odd Spot Club *89 Bold Street*

Odeon Cinema *London Road*

Royal Iris Cruiseship *River Mersey*

ELSEWHERE IN AND AROUND LIVERPOOL:

Aintree Institute *Longmoor Lane*

Albany Cinema *Northway, Maghull*

Blair Hall *Walton Road, Walton*

Casbah Coffee Club
8 Hayman's Green, West Derby

Childwall Labour Club

Finch Lane Social Club
Finch Lane, Nr Huyton

Gateacre Labour Club

Grafton Ballroom *West Derby Road*

Hambleton Hall *St. David's Road,
Page Moss, Nr Huyton*

Holyoake Hall
Smithdown Road, Nr Penny Lane

Knotty Ash Village Hall
East Prescot Road

Lee Park Golf Club
off Childwall Valley Road

Locarno Ballroom *West Derby Road*

Lowlands Club
Hayman's Green, West Derby

Morgue Skiffle Cellar
25 Oakhill Park, Broadgreen

Mossway Hall *Moss Way, Croxteth*

New Cabaret Artistes
174a Upper Parliament Street

New Clubmoor Hall (*Conservative Club*), *Back Broadway*

New Colony Club *80 Berkley Street*

Pavilion Theatre *Lodge Lane*

Picton Road Bus Depot Social Club
Picton Road, Wavertree

Quarry Bank High School
Harthill Road

Rialto Ballroom
Upper Parliament Street, Toxteth

Roseberry Street *Toxteth*

St.Barnabas Church Hall *Penny Lane*

St.John's Hall
Snaefell Avenue, Tuebrook

St.Peter's Church
Church Road, Woolton

Stanley Abattoir Social Club
East Prescot Road, Old Swan

Starline Club *Windsor Street, Toxteth*

25 Upton Green *Speke*

Wilson Hall *Speke Road, Garston*

Winter Gardens Ballroom
Heald Street, Garston

Woolton Village Club
Allerton Road, Woolton

CROSBY/SEAFORTH/LITHERLAND/BOOTLE:

Alexandra Hall *College Road, Crosby*

Lathom Hall *Lathom Avenue, Seaforth*

Litherland Town Hall
Hatton Hill Road, Litherland

St.John's Hall *Oriel Road, Bootle*

St.Luke's,*Crosby Church Youth Club*

ST HELENS/WIDNES:

Plaza Ballroom *Duke Street, St Helens*

Queen's Hall *Widnes*

SOUTHPORT:

ATC Club *Birkdale, Nr Southport*

Cambridge Hall *Lord Street*

Floral Hall *Promenade*

Glenpark Club *Lord Street*

Kingsway Club *Promenade*

Little Theatre *Hoghton Street*

Odeon Cinema *Lord Street*

Queens Hotel *Promenade*

WIRRAL:

Barnston Women's Institute
Barnston Road, Heswall

Ellesmere Port Civic Hall
Whitby Road, Ellesmere Port

Grosvenor Ballroom
Grosvenor Street, Wallasey

Haig Dance Club
Haig Avenue, Moreton

Hulme Hall *Port Sunlight Village*

Macdona Hall/Thistle Cafe
Banks Road, West Kirby

Majestic Ballroom
Conway Street, Birkenhead

Neston Institute *Hinderton Rd, Neston*

Newton Dancing School
Village Hall, Thingwall Road, Irby

St.Paul's Presbyterian Church Hall
North Road, Tranmere

Technical College Hall,
Borough Road, Birkenhead

Tower Ballroom
Promenade, New Brighton

YMCA *Whetstone Lane, Birkenhead*

YMCA *Birkenhead Road, Hoylake*

Victoria Hall *Village Road, Higher Bebington.*

1. Penny Lane

2. Strawberry Field –
Beaconsfield Road,
Woolton

3. John meets Paul for the
first time –
St Peter's Church, Woolton

4. Mathew Street –
Cavern Quarter

BEATLE BIRTHPLACES

5. John's birthplace –
Maternity Hospital, Oxford Street

6. Paul's birthplace –
Walton Hospital, Rice Lane

7. George's birthplace –
12 Arnold Grove, Wavertree

8. Ringo's birthplace –
9 Madryn Street, Dingle

BEATLE HOUSES

9. John's house 'Mendips' –
251 Menlove Avenue, Woolton

10. Paul's house –
20 Forthlin Road, Allerton

11. George's house –
174 Macket's Lane, Hunts Cross

12. Ringo's house –
10 Admiral Grove, Dingle

13. Pete Best's house & Casbah Club –
8 Hayman's Green, West Derby

14. Stu Sutcliffe's house –
37 Aigburth Drive, Sefton Park

15. Brian Epstein's house –
197 Queen's Drive, Woolton

BEATLE COLLEGES

16. John's College of Art –
Hope Street

17. Paul and George's college –
Liverpool Institute, Mount Street

18. John's College –
Quarry Bank Grammar School,
Harthill Road, Woolton

OTHER PLACES

19 John, Paul, George and Ringo play
together for the first time as the
Beatles – Hulme Hall, Port Sunlight
Village, Wirral

20. Birthplace of local Beatlemania –
Litherland Town Hall

> *To complete the picture, visit
> 'The Beatles Story' at Albert Dock.*

1. Birthplace –
Maternity Hospital, Oxford Street

2. House –
'Mendips', 251 Menlove Avenue,
Woolton

3. Strawberry Field Salvation
Army Children's Home –
Beaconsfield Road, Woolton

4. Infants and Junior School –
Dovedale Road, Penny Lane

5. College – Quarry Bank,
Harthill Road, Woolton

6. Liverpool College of Art –
Hope Street

7. John's first meeting with Paul
St Peter's Church Hall,
Woolton

8. John marries Cynthia –
Mount Pleasant Registry Office
Liverpool City Centre

9. First house –
9 Newcastle Road, Penny Lane

10. Mother's house –
1 Blomfield Road, Allerton

You can take the boys out of Liverpool but you can't take Liverpool out of the boys. From their first tentative efforts as budding songwriters, Lennon and McCartney were inspired by Liverpool, its people and its places. First-time visitors to the city are often surprised to find that there really is a Penny Lane and a Strawberry Field (but not an Abbey Road...that's in London!).

Here are songs that had their origins in, or were inspired by, Liverpool, the Beatles' birthplace. The album on which it appears is given after each song.

Cayenne (Anthology)

A Shadows-style instrumental written by Paul at Forthlin Road when he was about 14. This was before he met John and not long after he'd got his first guitar.

Do You Want to Know a Secret? (Please Please Me)

Written by John after he and Cynthia moved into Brian Epstein's flat at 36 Faulkner Street (above) this song has its foundation in another tune his mother sang to him as a young boy. "Want to know a secret? Promise not to tell?" warbled Snow White in the 1937 Disney classic *Snow White and the Seven Dwarfs*. The actual secret was John's realisation that he really was in love with Cynthia. The song provided Liverpudlian Billy J Kramer with a No. 1 hit in 1962.

John re-wrote the fairytale for his *Spaniard in the Works* book calling it *Snore Wife and the Several Dwarts*.

Eleanor Rigby (Revolver)

A number of theories have been put forward to explain the origins of the name Eleanor Rigby. Paul, who wrote the song, thought that 'Eleanor' came from Eleanor Bron the actress who appeared in the Beatles' *Help* whilst 'Rigby' was part of a sign 'Rigby & Evens Ltd', a firm of wine and spirit shippers he had noticed during a visit to Bristol. A more whimsical but unconfirmed explanation is that, perhaps subconsciously, Paul had seen the gravestone of the Eleanor Rigby who is buried in the churchyard of St Peter's Church, Woolton. The gravestone is just yards away from where Paul had first met John.

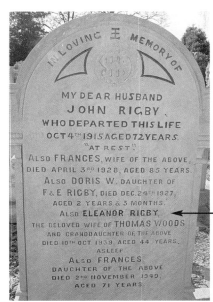

Free as a Bird *(Anthology)*

Based on a rough demo recorded by John in his New York apartment in 1977, this became the first 'new' Beatle record for 25 years. John's line – "Whatever happened to the boy that I once knew." – fits in with the concept that the song was written for a planned musical about John's life and times in the 60's.

The recording was treated by Paul, George and Ringo as though John was still alive. Paul explained, "We came up with this holiday scenario. I rang up Ringo and said let's pretend that John's gone on holiday and he's sent us a cassette and said, 'Finish it up for me'."

Directed by Joe Pytka, produced by Vincent Jolier, and principally filmed at various location around Liverpool, the *Free as a Bird*

The 'Free as a Bird' video shows a white grand piano falling from the sky and hurtling past Liverpool's most famous building, the Royal Liver.

video bristles with intriguing references to Beatle places and songs, including *Penny Lane*, *Strawberry Fields*, *Eleanor Rigby*, *Yellow Submarine* and *I am the Walrus*.

Golden Slumbers *(Abbey Road)*

Conceived by Paul on the piano at the house that he bought his father in Baskervyle Road, Heswall. A songbook belonging to his step-sister Ruth provided the inspiration. It contained the traditional lullaby *Golden Slumbers* by Shakespeare's contemporary, Thomas Dekker. As Paul was unable to read sheet music in those days, he made up his own melody.

Glass Onion *(The Beatles)*

Written by John to wind up all those fans who tried to outdo each other by finding hidden meanings in Beatle songs (remember the 'Paul is dead' theory?). Apart from Strawberry Fields, another Liverpool place-name is mentioned – the cast iron shore or, as we call it, 'The cassie'. To describe it as a 'beach', however, would be to over-glamourise it. It was, and is, pretty disgusting but as it was the only part of Liverpool's shoreline accessible to the public, it was popular with children from south Liverpool.

Hello Little Girl *(Anthology)*

John's first original song written when he was about 18. It was influenced by Buddy Holly's *Maybe Baby* and inspired by a song sung to him by his mother, a Cole Porter number *It's de-lovely* sung by Bob Hope. The song also gave another Liverpool group, The Fourmost, a number 7 hit in 1962.

Hey Jude *(The Beatles 1967-70)*

Written by Paul, it was about John and Cynthia's Liverpool-born five-year old son Julian ('Hey Jules' became 'Hey Jude') with whom Paul had always been close. John said that this was his favourite Paul song.

I Am The Walrus *(Magical Mystery Tour)*

The catalyst for this surreal song was a letter from a pupil at John's old school, Quarry Bank, explaining that his class had been given the task of analysing the lyrics of Beatle songs. John found this ironic especially as his English teachers had given up on him...Lennon had excelled only in class anarchy. The title was inspired by the poem *The Walrus and the Carpenter* written by John's favourite author, Lewis Carroll.

The line 'I am the eggman' may have been a reference to another Lewis Carroll character, Humpty Dumpty from *Through The Looking Glass*. Another line 'Yellow matter custard dripping from a dead dog's eye' came from a playground ditty chanted by every Liverpool schoolboy in the 40's, and usually directed at more sensitive souls i.e. girls! – 'Yellow matter custard, green snot pie, all mixed up with a dead dog's eye. Spread it on a butty, spread it on thick, then wash it down with a cup of cold sick.'

(Top) Wavertree Clock Tower and former Abbey Cinema. (Inset) Liverpool tram, Pier Head. (Bottom) The 'Dockers' Umbrella' – the Overhead Railway.

I Lost My Little Girl

Thought to be the earliest song written by Paul. It formed part of the Quarry Men's repertoire but was dropped when the group became the Beatles.

I'll Follow The Sun *(Beatles For Sale)*

An early Paul song written it is said when he was 16 and recovering from a bout of 'flu; the inspiration for the song came as he gazed through the lace-curtained front window of his Forthlin Road home.

I'll Get You *(With The Beatles)*

Another song written at 251 Menlove Avenue by John and Paul. It was the 'B' side of their mega-hit *She Loves You*.

In My Life *(Rubber Soul)*

As the original scribbled lyrics reveal, this song started life as an autobiographical reflection on some of John's favourite Liverpool landmarks as he travelled from Menlove Avenue to the Pier Head. Among the places he remembered were Penny Lane, Church Road (a road that leads from Penny Lane past Newcastle Road where his first home was) and the Clock Tower (Wavertree Clock Tower). "In the circle of the Abbey. I have seen some happy hours.", is a reference to the former Abbey Cinema. "Past the tramsheds with no trams." refers to the Smithdown Road Tram Depot. "On the 5 'bus into town" is the number 5 bus that goes from Woolton, past John's house and on to Liverpool city centre (Liverpudlians have always called their city centre 'town'). "Past the Duchy (a small cafe and hangout for local teenagers) and St Columba's" (church) "To the dockers umbrella that they pulled down." relates to one of the real wonders of Liverpool and a world-first for the city that was sadly demolished in the 1950's, an overhead electric railway that ran the length of Liverpool docks from Seaforth in the north past the Pier Head finishing at Dingle (near Ringo's home) in the south. Dockers on their way to and from work would shelter under it from the rain.

John's boyhood friend, Pete Shotton, claimed John told him that when he wrote the line – "...friends I still can recall, some are dead and some are living,.." he was specifically thinking about former Beatle Stu Sutcliffe and Pete.

I Saw Her Standing There (Please Please Me)

Refined by Paul and John in the front room of Paul's house in Forthlin Road, (above), the song's raw beginnings came to Paul as he was driving home one night in 1962. The lyrics were jotted down in a Liverpool Institute exercise book with Paul starting the ball rolling – "She was just seventeen" with John adding the very Liverpudlian saying – "You know what I mean."

Apparently, the inspiration for this song was Iris Caldwell, sister of Alan Caldwell, better known as Rory Storm, leader of Rory Storm and the Hurricanes whose drummer was Ringo Starr. Iris was a professional dancer and was 17 at the time Paul spotted her dancing the twist in her fishnet stockings at the Tower Ballroom, New Brighton. Paul and Iris dated on and off for a few years.

I Call Your Name (With The Beatles)

Although Paul claims to remember working on this song in John's bedroom, John reckoned that he wrote it before he was in the Quarry Men or the Beatles.

In Spite of All the Danger (Anthology)

Written by Paul, with a guitar solo by George. Influenced by Elvis Presley, it has two claims to fame. It was the embryo Beatles very first record, made in 1958 in Percy Phillips' small studio in Kensington, Liverpool, for less than £1. Also, it was the only original song performed by the Quarry Men at that time.

Julia (The Beatles)

Although Julia was directed at his mother, John is also telling her that he has found a new love – 'ocean child' (Yoko in Japanese). As Paul said of Julia – "...John absolutely adored her, and not just because she was his mum." Written by John during his latter Beatle days, this gentle song couldn't be more different than Mother.

Like Dreamers Do (Anthology)

An early Paul number which became part of the Quarry Men's and then the Beatles' repertoire until 1962.

Love Me Do (Please Please Me)

Written by Paul whilst sagging off school. John's main contribution was the middle eight and the distinctive harmonica solo. John had played the mouth organ since childhood and had admired Delbert McClinton's harmonica work on Bruce Channel's Hey Baby. John was to meet him at the Tower Ballroom in New Brighton a few months before the Beatles recorded Love Me Do and Delbert generously showed him his technique. Love Me Do is also memorable because producer George Martin wasn't happy with new boy Ringo's drumming and replaced him on the recording with session drummer Andy White.

Maggie May *(Let It Be)*

The final 'throw-away' track on the *Let It Be* album, *Maggie May* is a well-known Liverpool folk song about a local prostitute who plied her trade along Lime Street, one of the main streets in the city centre. The song was a hit for the Vipers during the mid-50's skiffle boom and formed part of the Quarry Men's repertoire.

Liverpool-Welsh playwrite Alun Owen, who's success with the play *No Trams To Lime Street*, led to him writing the screenplay for the Beatles' first film *A Hard Day's Night*, went on to write the musical *Maggie May* with composer Lionel Bart.

Michelle *(Rubber Soul)*

Largely written by Paul, the song had its origins in a party piece with which he amused his, and John's art college, friends. Jan Vaughan, the wife of Ivan Vaughan, who introduced his school-friend Paul McCartney to John Lennon, was a French teacher and helped Paul out with the lyrics, coming up with the girl's name – 'Michelle, ma belle' – and the line – 'sont les mots qui vont tres bien ensemble' ('These are words that go together well').

Mother *(Imagine)*

The opening song on John's solo album *Imagine*. The song's gut-wrenching intensity is almost too painful to listen to. Julia was the mother he lost twice – once at the age of five when Julia handed him over to her sister Mimi to look after and again at the age of 17 when she was killed in a road accident outside Mimi's house. The song opens with the disquieting sound of a funeral church bell (church bells were rooted in John's childhood – "Sundays, I heard church bells") and ends with John screaming over and over again – "Mummy don't go. Daddy come home."

My Mummy's Dead *(Imagine)*

The closing song on John's *Imagine* album with the death of his beloved mother Julia again as its theme.

Norwegian Wood *(Rubber Soul)*

John's said that he wrote this song about an affair he'd had whilst at the same time trying to prevent his wife Cynthia finding out about it. John's friend and fellow Quarry Man, Pete Shotton, thought that the song harked back to John's student days in the Gambier Terrace flat (left) he shared with Stu Sutcliffe, specifically the reference to sleeping in the bath and John's practice of burning wooden furniture in the fireplace.

One After 909 *(Let It Be)*

Written by John in 1957, probably in Paul's house at Forthlin Road. Paul elaborated: – We used to sag off school, go back to my house and the two of us would write. There are a lot of songs from back then that we've never reckoned on because they're all very unsophisticated songs...We hated the words to *One After 909*."

Penny Lane *(Magical Mystery Tour)*

Although John had first mentioned Penny Lane in the original draft of *In My Life*, it was Paul who wrote this nostalgic song. When Liverpudlians refer to 'Penny Lane' they mean the general area that has the Penny Lane 'roundabout' as its focus. Penny Lane itself is a narrow road that leads from the University of Liverpool's Halls of Residence at Greenbank to its junction with Smithdown Road and Allerton Road. For the first five years of his life John lived 'in' Penny Lane – although his home was just around the corner in Newcastle Road.

Suburban and mundane though it may appear in real life, Penny Lane is a 'must see' for all Beatle fans visiting Liverpool. The barber's shop is still there although Mr Bioletti, the barber who gave John, Paul and George their 'short back and sides' haircuts when they were children, isn't. The bank is there too and so is the shelter in the middle of the roundabout. Originally a bus shelter, it has been converted into the Sgt Pepper's Bistro. Further along Allerton Road at its junction with Mather Avenue is the local fire station.

Explaining how the song was written, John said simply – "It was just reliving childhood."

Please Please Me (Please Please Me)
Many of John's musical influences came from his mother Julia and the songs she sang to him as a child. A Bing Crosby hit in the early 30's, Please was one such song. A born wordsmith, John was intrigued with the line – 'Oh please, lend your little ears to my pleas.' and its twin meanings of the words 'please' and 'pleas'.

Please Please Me was written by John in his bedroom at 251 Menlove Avenue.

The 'shelter in the middle of the roundabout'   St Barnabus Church   Penny Lane   Bank   Barber shop

He recalled – "I remember the day and the pink eyelet on the bed." (he probably meant 'coverlet', a bedspread). He'd also been influenced by Roy Orbison's *Only The Lonely* and pictured him singing *Please Please Me* – the original version of John's song was much slower.

Polythene Pam *(Abbey Road)*

Written and sung by John – "...I used a thick Liverpool accent because it was supposed to be about a mythical Liverpool scrubber dressed up in her jackboots and kilt." There was in fact a young girl fan of the Beatles called Pat from their Cavern days who, unbelievably, had a bizarre habit of eating polythene. She was known to the Beatles as Polythene Pat. Subsequently, John claimed that the song related to an incident when a friend involved him in a threesome with a girl dressed in polythene!

PS I Love You *(Please Please Me)*

Mainly written by Paul with some help from John after Paul's girlfriend Dot Rhone visited him in Hamburg. Head over heels in love with Paul, she assumed that he had her in mind when writing this 1962 song, a supposition Paul later denied, explaining that he never had any specific girl in mind. Paul ended their relationship that summer at 93 Garmoyle Road, the flat she shared with John's girlfriend, Cynthia.

Step Inside Love *(Anthology)*

The Beatles' association with the Liverpool singer and entertainer Cilla Black stretched back to the days when she was a cloakroom attendant at the Cavern club. Fitting therefore that Paul should write this as the theme song for her new TV series *Cilla* in 1968. She also recorded two other songs – *Love of the Loved*, an old Quarry Men's song that became her first single, and Paul's *It's for You*.

Strawberry Fields Forever *(Magical Mystery Tour)*

John regarded this as his favourite Beatle song. Like Penny Lane, Strawberry Field (below) is a real place close to where John lived in Menlove Avenue. In fact he could get there from his back garden. The wooded grounds

of this Salvation Army children's home were familiar territory to John and his schoolfriends as they climbed trees and played hide and seek amongst the bushes.

Reputedly, although Paul has denied it, this was the first song on a new album that was to be autobiographical and would develop the Liverpool themes hinted at in songs such as *In My Life* and *Eleanor Rigby*. The concept was abandoned in favour of the *Sgt Pepper* album and *Strawberry Fields* and *Penny Lane* were issued as a single.

the song and thought that John was referring to himself as the working class hero. In fact, John had been brought up in the green and gentile suburb of Woolton in a house that still has the buzzer system with which the master or mistress could summon the domestic help. And John had never done a conventional day's work in his life.

Yellow Submarine *(Yellow Submarine)*
The title song of the Beatles' animated film was written by Paul as a children's song to be sung by Ringo. During visits to Merseyside when he had young children

When I'm 64 *(Sgt. Pepper's Lonely Hearts Club Band)*
Written in the style of the 20's and 30's songs played by Paul's father in his days heading the Jim Mac Band, it was released when Paul's dad was in fact 64. However, it was composed much earlier on the family piano in Forthlin Road when Paul was about 15.

Working Class Hero *(Imagine)*
John's cynical, world-weary song from his *Imagine* album is firmly grounded in his school and college days in Liverpool. Many people misunderstood

of his own, Paul and family would sing *Yellow Submarine* as they travelled under the river through the Mersey Tunnel.

The remixed songtrack and digitally enhanced film were premiered at the Philharmonic Hall, Liverpool, on 14 September 1999.

You'll Be Mine *(Anthology)*
Made in 1960 on a borrowed tape recorder in Paul's house, it is noteworthy only because it was the first recording of a Lennon and McCartney song.

DAY TRIPPER

1. Albert Dock Pier Head – Liverpool's top visitor attraction includes three 'must sees' – the Merseyside Maritime Museum (actually three museums in one) – also incorporates the HM Customs & Excise National Museum, and the Museum of Liverpool Life (*Tel: 0151 478 4499*); the Tate Gallery Liverpool displays works from the National Collection of Modern Art (*Tel: 0151 702 7400*) and there's the Beatles Story (*Tel: 0151 709 1963*) as well as shops, restaurants, cafes, bars and pubs. The largest group of Grade 1 Listed buildings in Britain and the U.K's most popular heritage attraction with around four million visitors each year. There is also a budget Holiday Inn Express Hotel and a Howard Johnson Hotel is due to open in 2001.

The Albert Dock complex is open every day of the year except Christmas Day from 10am. General admission is free and there is ample free parking.

Enquiries – Tourist Information Centre, Albert Dock. *Tel: 0151-708 8854* Website: *www.albertdock.com*

2. Mersey Ferries
Immortalised in the *Ferry 'cross the Mersey* song by Gerry and the Pacemakers and a feature on the river for more than 700 years. Without doubt the very best way of seeing Liverpool's spectacular waterfront. Hourly sight-seeing cruises throughout the day starting from the Pier Head with pick-up points on the Wirral at Seacombe (Wallasey) and Woodside (Birkenhead).

Without doubt a trip on a Mersey Ferry captures the essence of Liverpool – definitely an experience not to be missed, whatever the weather.

Enquiries – *Tel: 0151-630 1030*
Website: *www.merseyferries.co.uk*

3. Liverpool Cathedral Hope Street.
Largest Anglican Cathedral in Europe with tallest gothic arches ever built. Architect was Sir Giles Gilbert Scott who also designed Britain's famous red telephone boxes. Great views from atop the tower. Open daily 8am to 6pm.

Enquiries – *Tel: 0151-709 6271*

4. Metropolitan Cathedral of Christ the King Mount Pleasant.
A 'modern classic' completed in 1967. Spectacular lantern contains 2,000 pieces of stained glass and can be seen to most dramatic effect from the inside on a sunny day. Open daily 8am to 6pm (5pm winter).

Enquiries – *Tel: 0151-709 9222*

5. Walker Art Gallery
William Brown Street.
One of the world's top art museums housing the largest collection of paintings in England outside London. Renowned for its European paintings and sculpture from 1300 to the present day. Open Mon to Sat 10am to 5pm; Sun 12 noon to 5pm.

Enquiries – *Tel: 0151-478 4199*
Website: *www.nmgm.org.uk*

The famous Liver Bird, to be seen atop the Royal Liver Building at the Pier Head and adorning numerous other city buildings, has been a powerful symbol of Liverpool dating back many centuries.

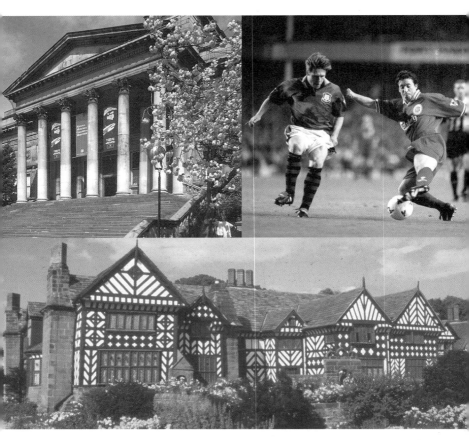

6. *Liverpool Museum,* William Brown St. Apart from an aquarium, vivarium, Natural History Centre and Planetarium, this large museum houses treasures from civilisations past and present. The museum is undergoing a major transformation so expect disruption. Open Mon to Sat 10am to 5pm; Sun 12 noon to 5pm.

Enquiries – *Tel: 0151-478 4399*
Website: *www.nmgm.org.uk*

7. *Speke Hall,* The Walk, Speke, Liverpool 24
(7 miles from city centre). Situated in beautiful grounds near the airport, this is one of the most famous Elizabethan manor houses in the country. Its owners, the National Trust, operate tours from here to Paul McCartney's former home in Forthlin Road.

Enquiries – *Tel: 0151-427 7231*
Website: *www.nationaltrust.org.uk*

8. *Liverpool and Everton Football Clubs.* It has been said that soccer on Merseyside is a matter of life and death. In fact, it is much more important than that! Behind the scenes tours of both clubs take place throughout the year (LFC: Daily 10am to 5pm/EFC: Sun, Mon, Wed and Fri at 11am and 2pm).

Enquiries:
Liverpool F.C. *Tel: 0151-260 6677*
Website: *www.liverpoolfc.net*
Everton F.C. *Tel: 0151-330 2266*
Website: *www.evertonfc.com*

9. *Croxteth Hall and Country Park*
Muirhead Avenue East, Liverpool
(5 miles from city centre). 500 acre country estate, once the ancestral home of the Earls of Sefton. Edwardian house, walled garden, Home Farm etc.

Enquiries: *Tel: 0151-228 5311*
Website: *www.croxteth.co.uk*

10. *Liverpool City Centre.*
Just enjoy the bustling, vibrant city centre with its excellent choice of theatres, cinemas, pubs, wine bars, restaurants and shops, including the Cavern Walks, Clayton Square and St. John's Shopping Centres. Don't miss Bluecoat Chambers, School Lane (Enquiries: *Tel: 0151-709 5689*). A beautiful and peaceful oasis in the heart of the busy shopping centre, this Queen Anne building dates from 1717 making it the oldest building in the city centre. There's an art gallery, cafe, craft gallery, regular events, etc.

For a great night out head for the Albert Dock, Mathew Street, Concert Square/ Slater Street, Hardman Street or Queen Square areas. This is where you will find the greatest concentration of pubs, clubs and restaurants.

For information about these and other places to visit and things to see and do in Liverpool and elsewhere on Merseyside contact the Tourist Information Centres at Queen Square or Albert Dock (details on next page).

Tourist information
(including accommodation bookings):

Queen Square Centre
Open Mon-Sat 9.00am to 5.30pm (Tues
from 10.00am. Sun and Bank Holidays
10.30am to 4.30pm)
UK callers – *Tel: 0906 680 6886 (calls
cost 25p per minute)* /Overseas callers
Tel: +44 151 709 5111
e-mail: *askme@visitliverpool.com*

Tourist Information Centre, Albert Dock
Open daily 10.00am to 5.30pm
Tel: 0151-708 8838

Short break/accommodation bookings:
UK callers – *Tel 0845 601 1125* (local call
rate). Overseas callers – *+44 151 709 8111*
Website: *www.visitliverpool.com*

Beatles Car Tours:

Bookings – Tel: official BeatleGuides
Hilary Oxlade *0151 931 3075 or 0780
3206 599* or Sylvia McMurtry *0151 707
9313 or 0771 511 5225*. Japanese
visitors looking for a Japanese speaking

official BeatleGuide can contact Takuje
Abe – *Tel: 0151 220 9543*.

Beatles Magical Mystery Tours:

A two-hour Beatles 'Magical Mystery
Tour' departs daily from the Queen
Square Centre at 12.10pm and 2.40pm
with pick-ups at The Beatles Story at
12.30pm and 3pm. Finishes at the
Cavern club. Information/bookings:
Tel: 0151-236 9091 or 709 3285

City Sightseeing Tour:

One-hour City Sightseeing Coach Tour
of all the major points of interest in
Liverpool City Centre. Times/frequency
vary. *Enquiries – Tel: 0151 933 2324 or
'phone Tourist Info on 0906 680 6886
(calls cost 25p per minute)*.

Travel:

General information about travel within
Merseyside, including Merseyrail:
'phone the Merseytravel Line – *0151-
236 7676* (daily from 8am to 8pm)

Airports –
Liverpool Airport – *Tel: 0151-288 4444*
Manchester Airport – *Tel: 0161-489 3000*

Ambulance – *Tel: 999* and ask for *'Ambulance'*

Breakdown –
Automobile Association (AA) – Breakdown: *Tel: 0800 887766*; Information – *Tel: 0345 500600*
Royal Automobile Club (RAC) – Breakdown: – *Tel: 0800 828282*; Information – *Tel: 0151-709 7979*

British Transport Police, Lime Street Station – *Tel: 0151-709 2120*

Emergencies only (Police, Ambulance, Fire) – *Tel: 999*

Emergency Medical – Royal Liverpool Hospital (Casualty) *Tel: 0151-706 2000*

Emergency Dental – Royal Liverpool Dental Hospital – *Tel: 0151-709 0141*

Mersey Ferries – *Tel: 0151-630 1030*

National Express, Norton Street Coach Station (Information/bookings – *Tel: 0990 80 80 80*)

Passport Office – India Buildings, Water Street (open 9am to 4pm Mon-Fri) *Tel: 0151-471 2700*

Police – Cop Shop, Church Street *Tel: 0151-709 6010*

Post Offices (City Centre) – St John's Centre / Lyceum, Bold Street / India Buildings, Brunswick Street.

Rail: enquiries – *Tel: 0345 484950*
Left luggage – Lime Street main train station open daily 7am-10pm.

Sea – Seacat services between Isle of Man and Dublin *(Tel: 0870 523 523)*. For services between Belfast and Liverpool – *Tel: 01532 779090*

Money: (Liverpool City Centre)

Banking/bureau de change services:

Barclays, Whitechapel

Lloyds, Great Charlotte Street

Midland, Bold Street

National Westminster, Renshaw Street

Royal Bank of Scotland, Dale Street

TSB, Church Street

Bureau de change/travel services:

Thomas Cook, 75 Church Street
Tel: 0151-709 3845

American Express, 54 Lord Street
Tel: 0151-708 9202

Queen Square Tourist Information Centre *Tel: 0906 680 6886*

Albert Dock Tourist Information Centre *Tel: 0151-708 8854*

T

U

V

W

Y

Picture credits

The late Bill Connell (Peter Kaye) – 3, 11(top), 14(bottom), 16, 19(bottom), 33(bottom), 34(top), 41(bottom), 49(top), 50, 57(top & circled), 66(bottom), 69(top), 84(bottom), 85, 86,
Liverpool City Council – 6, 15,
Liverpool Echo – 10, 11(bottom), 12,(bottom), 25(right), 62(top left, bottom)
Don Valentine – 38(top right), 81
David Oxtoby – 42(right)
Ann Mason – 43(right)
Geoff Rhind – 46/64(top)
The late Graham Spencer – 78(bottom)
Tex O'Hara – 80(top),
Leslie Kearney – 84(top)
LFC – 98(top right)
Maurice Cockrill – 54(top), 60(top)
EMI Records Ltd – 61(bottom left)

With the exception of a small number of photographs whose ownership is not known to me (I would be pleased to give due acknowledgement in future editions), all location and other photographs are the copyright of Ron Jones.